The System

How to Get Laid *TODAY*!

by Roy Valentine

ROY VALENTINE

For information, contact:
www.eyecontactmedia.com
info@eyecontactmedia.com

Cover Illustration Photo: Suze Randall www.suze.net

"The 1% Rule" is a trademark of Eye Contact Media, Inc.
All trademarks and copyrights mentioned in this book are
the properties of their respective owners.

ISBN-10: 0-9729187-1-X
ISBN-13: 978-0-9729187-1-8

Printed in the USA

Dedicated

*To all the ladies -
You are the only proof
I need of God's perfection --*

*because
only a perfect being
could create such perfection
that we call WOMAN!*

————————

*Thanks for sharing your passion, your beauty,
your secrets.*

Thanks for a great game!

ACKNOWLEDGEMENTS

To the Players

Sylvie, Mike, Keith, Errol, Dave, Lisa, Sanjay, Binh, Angie

Thanks for your support with this quest.

The System

Introduction

Here are three important questions men all over the world would like answered:

1. Is there a process, a technique, or a system that the average guy can use to get laid any day of the week without the need for wealth, fame, or good looks?

2. Is it possible to take home girls and have sex with them within minutes after you first lay eyes on them?

3. Are there men out there who possess this skill, this know-how that seems to elude most other men?

This book not only answers these critical questions asked by men everywhere in the world, but it actually gives step-by-step instructions and real life examples on how to achieve these goals.

This is not a book about romance, relationships, or how to find the woman of your dreams. These things may happen as a result of this book, but they aren't a big concern for most men. This book is about *changing your life* by learning how to achieve one goal dear to men everywhere: getting laid TODAY. It teaches you how to identify the right woman, seduce her, take her home, and have sex with her within minutes of seeing her for the first time.

Instead of suffering through the pain of rejection, doubt, and loneliness you will now walk confidently knowing that you can have sex whenever you like. Instead of begging women for sex, you will control when, with whom, and how often you have sex. Instead of wondering if she likes you, you will know exactly what to do to take her home. Instead of wasting time and money on dates, you will take her home minutes after meeting her.

The System technique is simple. Everyone can do it! And the more you do, the better you become. The game therefore changes from 'how to get laid' to 'how to manage all these women you have sex with.'

The goal of the System is to help men and women improve the quality of their lives by having more sex with a better selection of partners. This is done by helping men build their confidence by learning how to identify, meet, and take home amazingly sexy women.

The System creates an environment where both men and women benefit. By understanding the signals that women constantly project and knowing exactly how to follow up on these signals, men can now respond to the women that want them to respond, instead of 'hitting on' women that have no interest in them.

Women benefit from the System because now the man will *know*! Every woman wants a man who just knows exactly what to do without having to tell him. From reading this book, you can become that man!

Table of Contents

Chapter 1 Unlimited Possibilities   11

Chapter 2 Confidence–the Mental Game   23
The Thoughts that Limit Men's Confidence   27
The Top Reasons Girls Sleep With Guys   38

Chapter 3 Scoping   47
What's the 1% Rule   50
The Three Categories of Girls   53
The Girl Game   63

Chapter 4 Making Contact   91
The Introduction   95
Women's Body Language   98

Chapter 5 Establish Connection   111
How to Flirt with Really Beautiful Girls   119

Chapter 6 Close the Deal   133

Chapter 7 Closing on Dates   157

Chapter 8 How to be a Player   185
Rules of the Player   200

The 5 Steps to Success

CONFIDENCE
- Thoughts that limit you
- Top reasons why girls sleep with men

SCOPING
- Scan target area
- Identify target
- Confirm target

MAKE CONTACT
- Proximity
- Introduction
- Confirm interest

ESTABLISH CONNECTION
- Achieve comfort level
- Achieve trust
- Confirm interest

CLOSE THE DEAL
- The invitation
- The seduction
- Home run

I had no translators and had never seen the girls before, yet within minutes of meeting, we were on our way back to my apartment or hotel.

Chapter 1
Unlimited Possibilities

Do men get laid because of luck or skill?

Only five steps are required to pick up a girl and get her into bed. Amazingly, this simple process works anywhere in the world, with any girl. I've personally tested it in over 20 countries and five continents—even places where I didn't speak the language. I had no translators and had never seen the girls before, yet within *minutes* of meeting, we were on our way back to my apartment or hotel. Some places where I've picked up girls in minutes using this system include: France, the USA,

Rome, Prague, Hungary, Japan, Singapore, Sweden, Denmark, Germany, Holland, Thailand, Hong Kong, and the Caribbean, to name a few. In fact, in most cases I know that I'll be able to take home the girl and have sex with her even ***before*** I speak with her.

I say this not to impress you but to impress upon you the possibilities of what you will learn from this book. Now, I know some of you must be thinking 'that's impossible' or 'he paid for it,' but it *is* possible, and I am fundamentally against paying for sex. I have no moral issues with prostitution, but paying for sex takes the sport out of the game of getting laid, and I happen to love the sport. You don't need money to get laid—what it takes is skill.

This is not a general book about how to get laid some day. The System provides specific instructions and examples of how to get laid *today*. Within these pages you'll learn how to identify girls who are ready and willing to go home with you right NOW, how to meet them, and how to close the deal within minutes of meeting them. I will also teach you the essential skills required to be a real Player. It's a fast, easy, and effective way of getting laid without spending a penny or leaving your house.

The steps are so simple that anyone can master them. I've taught this System to men and to lesbian and bisexual women. In all cases, their closure rate improved dramatically. The core principle is this: If you follow the System, you don't have to worry about getting rejected and you'll be able to take a girl home within minutes of meeting her.

How is this possible? It works because The System is both a science and a technology, and it's tried, tested, and proven. In fact, the definition of a system is: an organized set of interrelated ideas or principles. This System will change the life of any man by forever altering the dynamics of his interaction with women. Instead of making unfocused passes and getting rejected, he will have to turn women down or schedule them simply because he doesn't have enough time to pursue each opportunity.

What is the System and how was it developed?

The System is a structured process for picking up girls. It is a technology based on certain fundamental characteristics that can be found in everyone. I developed this method through observation and practice. I've spent my career developing various types of systems in computer technology and business. My experience with developing and teaching complex technical and business information has enabled me to simplify what seems like impossible concepts about picking up girls. Also, after being a nerd for many years (the lowest guy on the totem pole to get laid), I've been able to make this approach nerd-proof. Therefore, by following the System, even Bob from accounting or Eugene from the IT department will have more sex than they can handle.

I developed the System using a Rapid Implementation approach—in other words, figuring how do something in the fastest and most effective way possible. After years of field-testing and optimization, I produced a simple five-step process that can be used and repeated by anyone. The core belief is that any guy can get laid within minutes of meeting a girl. The trick is to pick the right girl and then follow the correct process to get that girl at home and in bed.

The results of mastering this approach are:

- No more dating. Why date her when you can take her home a few minutes after meeting her?

- Reduced cost. You don't need to spend money to get laid.
- Superior confidence. Your hardest task will be to schedule who you want to have sex with and when.
- No more rejections. You'll know if she's interested even before you start talking to her.
- Bragging rights. Every guy you know will be jealous of you and every girl will want to do you.

What makes the System different from other approaches?

It's quite fascinating that I've had lots of friends over the years that executed some of these ideas, but still couldn't close in a regular and consistent manner. In other words, they got some play but weren't able to close the deal. They may have tried Step 1 and Step 2, but didn't know Step 3. Some even got as far as Step 3 but didn't follow through with Step 4. Other guys mix up the steps or simply had no game at all.

Just hang out in a club until the doors close and you'll see guys falling to their knees and begging girls to go home with them. It's pathetic. The saddest cases spend the entire night kissing or feeling up a chick, only to be let down at 2:00 am when the place is closing. He stands in the doorway, watching her speed off with her girlfriend. This is all avoidable. Most painful of all is the man who just spent several hundred dollars and was convinced that he'd get *lucky*.

The System has nothing to do with luck. The System is about skill, and about learning a process that works all the time. It's about learning to spot the girl who will 'put out' that day, versus the ones who are looking for a free meal, free drinks, or ego boost before going home to a boyfriend or husband.

Many books have been published about getting laid. Here are some of the principles suggested by their authors:

- Be an asshole and you'll get laid.
- Get an expensive sports car and you'll get laid.
- Buy her lots of stuff and you'll get laid.
- Be her best friend, kiss her ass, hand your balls to her, and you'll get laid.

I agree that sometimes, some of these things will work, but you'll still be depending on LUCK. Also, with those approaches you'll be lucky if you get lucky once every few months. One approach even suggested taking weeks or months to reprogram yourself. Does that even make sense when you want to get laid today?

The System is based on principles used by top athletes everywhere. Michael Jordan and Tiger Woods' ability to always perform at a peak level has nothing to do with luck. They use a system for success. They have the ability, at will, to mentally condition themselves for success; identify an opportunity for the perfect shot; and they have the skill required to execute the perfect shot. This system allows top athletes to continuously perform at a peak level and to build the confidence required to sustain the peak. This system is repeated in each game and is optimized over time to near perfection by these athletes.

Likewise, The System is a formula for success that anyone can learn and use TODAY. The System is different because it has nothing to do with pickup lines or luck. You don't need to be wealthy or famous. You don't need to lie, get girls drunk, or be an asshole to get laid. You NEVER beg a chick for sex, you're always in control of the situation, and you will learn the confidence required for success. The System is a repeatable process you can use everywhere and anywhere. Follow The System and the possibilities are unlimited.

The girl was practically begging him to take her home, but he missed all the signals, he overlooked the body language.

What will you learn?

You will learn some basic rules. One of these is the 1% rule. It's critical in understanding why you should never have to spend a night alone. I'll explain it in Chapter 3. In fact, in each chapter you'll learn more than most guys will know their whole lives about how to get laid faster and more consistently than anyone you know.

But as vital as it is to learn what to do, it's also important to learn what *not* to do. I recently watched a friend who had everything set up perfectly. The girl was practically begging him to take her home, but he missed all the signals, he overlooked the body language. When we left the bar that night, I had a chick on my arms and he had none. When I inquired about why he hadn't asked the girl to go home with him, he said she wasn't interested. I was surprised, because she obviously wanted him. But he was clueless. He was shocked when I told him that I was sure she was interested. He wouldn't accept it. I turned to the beautiful stranger I hadn't known two hours before and ask her opinion. She confirmed that the girl was interested. He responded with the familiar "Oh no! Why didn't you tell me?" But it was too late.

As you read this book you'll learn to detect and respond to signals that girls put out consistently every minute of every day. You'll learn how and how not to approach a girl. You'll learn the reasons why girls say "yes" or 'no." I'll take the mystery out of getting laid and show you a process you can use wherever you are. You'll learn how to close the deal every time, without fear or rejection. If you don't believe this is possible then that's your first mistake. But don't worry; we'll handle that in Chapter 2.

Before you can get laid you have to get your head straight. Most guys don't stand a chance—not because of what they do, but because of how they think. They become their own worst enemies by leaving the girl with no other option but to say "no" or "get lost." The problem is YOU. No, you're not a bad person, but you sabotage yourself with the way you think, which is projected through the way you act.

Here's an example that happened with a buddy I used to hang with. He came from a foreign country and was convinced that girls from his country wouldn't put out on the first date. Even though I'd proved him wrong on different occasions, he always had a convenient excuse why he couldn't close with girls from his country.

One night we visited a local hot spot and spotted some girls who met our criteria. We went over and hooked it up with them. I worked the blonde and he worked the girl from his country. I was impressed because he really had his game on that night. I took off maybe an hour later with my pick. The next day I gave him a call, anxious to trade success stories. He told me how hot the girl was for him, but there was no point in asking her home because girls from his country would never go home with a guy they just met. He was able to get her phone number to call her in a few days. They dated a couple times and he spent a lot of money, but was never able to have sex with her. The challenge here was not the girl, but the rigid category he placed her in.

This cultural barrier happens often. I call it *The Virgin Mary Concept*. Certain girls, usually the race or culture of the guy, are often thought of as "*good girls*" and considered lifetime virgins without the promise of marriage or a relationship. We speak about categories for girls later in the book, but in a different context. You'll learn the real deal.

They will show no mercy.

This is exactly what women do.

A man's lack of confidence is

his greatest weakness and ...

Chapter 2
Confidence - the Mental Game

<u>**CONFIDENCE**</u>
- Thoughts that limit you
- Top reasons why girls sleep with men

What is the #1 reason why women reject men?

Well, let's get down to business. Step 1 is to have your mental game down. If you've ever played football and charged onto the field thinking you're going to lose or get hurt—guess what will happen? You'll get killed! The other team will instantly sense your fear and exploit it. They will show no mercy.

This is exactly what women do. A man's lack of confidence is his greatest weakness and the primary reason women will step on him. This is why a man will pay for her drinks, her girlfriend's drinks, her entry to the club, dinner, jewelry, clothes, and trips – and still never get laid. She uses this weakness against him. A confident man knows that he doesn't have to spend money to get laid.

How do you gain confidence? By getting your head together and improving your skills. Guys carry several limiting thoughts around as baggage. These thoughts affect the way they approach, speak to, and think of girls. Girls read these limiting thoughts as insecurity and lack of confidence. For instance, a man may believe he shouldn't try to kiss the girl because she's a good girl and will not kiss on the first date. The girl's interpretation of his lack of action is that he's not confident. Using body language, she may have been sending out signals that she wanted a kiss. Women communicate largely through body language and they expect men to understand their wants and needs without verbalizing them. Women believe when they give out these signals a confident, experienced man will take the appropriate actions. They expect this of men and will always choose the more confident man over the one who lacks confidence. They collectively refer to guys who lack confidence as wimps, nerds, or nice guys. The confident guy is often referred to as a bad boy, a jerk, or an asshole. But who gets laid whenever he wants? Not Mister Nice Guy!

Why? Not because he's nice, but because a woman sees him as someone without the confidence required to challenge or excite her. Without confidence, a man accepts every abuse or situation from a woman without challenging her – not realizing that he's being tested. He believes he has no control over whether or not he gets laid. He believes she has all the power. He believes that getting laid has to do with luck, wealth, or getting a girl drunk. A man without confidence is a man without skill. A man without skill is boring to a woman. She's a hunter, but the kill is too easy, so she moves on to the next challenge. She looks for the big game, the guy she can't control or possess.

Women are very good at this game. Their skills are instinctive and their methods ruthless. I love women and appreciate their ability to conquer and manipulate men. One can learn a lot from observing pros at their game. By observing these women at work, you'll learn that many of our beliefs about women are without basis. And these beliefs trap us. To be a good football player, one studies great football players; to be a good hunter, one study great hunters; to be a good player, one must study women. Think of it:

- A woman has sex whenever she wants to and makes the man feel that she has just done him a favor.
- Women cheat on their boyfriends and husbands, are rarely ever caught, and manage to keep the illusion of innocence with their partners.
- They eat and drink for free, and make guys feel like shit if they don't pay.
- They use sex to negotiate whatever they want and usually win.
- They've convinced men that the cost of sex is romance, and the definition of romance is the showering of women with expensive gifts.
- They've convinced guys that to be a 'real man' is to do whatever the woman wants.

What's the point of this? We must now challenge all the things we believe about women. These beliefs are like baggage that holds back our confidence. Until you're able to dump these beliefs, you won't be successful with picking up girls. Here are some of the thoughts that limit men's confidence and screws up their game.

The thoughts that limit men's confidence

1. She's a good girl and would never put out on the first date.
2. She's not that kind of girl.
3. She's married, or she has a boyfriend.
4. She's too hot. She could never want me.
5. I'm not buff enough or rich enough.
6. If I had sex with her I'd be using her or taking advantage of her.
7. We're friends and she doesn't think of me like that.
8. She's a friend of the family and would not be interested.
9. My cock isn't big enough.
10. She's black or white or Asian or Latin, or whatever, and I'm from a different culture, so she'd never be interested.

The list could go on and on. You should make a list for yourself and find ways to challenge these assumptions. They define your interaction with women and create massive limitations. These limitations must be cast away. Women will smell the fear and uncertainty and will go home with your best friend. Stop and take notice of the guys who get all the girls. See if they have this problem. These limitations are just negative thoughts you learned from your mom, your sister, the movies, books, etc. These are beliefs, not FACTS! The reality is different.

So what is the reality? That's an easy question. Talk to a female friend and ask her if she'd prefer to sit home on a Friday night or to be with a cool guy. She'll say, "Who'd want to stay home on a Friday night?" Next question. Ask that female friend if she believes that sleeping with a skilled, confident man means she's being used. Of course, you may have to describe what a good lover is, since many women have unfortunately not had that experience. So let me try to explain. A good lover is when a woman feels both physically and emotionally satisfied at the end of making love to a guy. A good lover is the man she wants to brag about to her girlfriends. A good lover is the man who'll surprise her with feeling she didn't know were possible. A good lover is the guy she may think she's falling in love with, but deep down inside she can't stop thinking about the sex. A good lover is the guy she'll want to posses, but she can't conquer. A good lover is her bad boy. He could be you.

So-called good girls, bad girls, and everyone in-between would like to meet men who can do this for them. With this, THEY feel lucky. But it's not luck—it's skill.

This is part of the System that's very important. Why have someone throw you the ball if you can't score a touchdown? The best quarterbacks perform consistently over and over and over, because they use a system that allows them to perform at a peak level each time, each game.

So what are you doing when you meet a girl, seduce her, and make passionate love to her? You're doing HER a favor. If she wasn't with you that moment, she might be at home fantasizing about meeting someone like you. Or worse, she'd be wasting her time with some girlfriend bitching about how there are no good men out there. You know it's true.

Now is the time to make the transition. It's time to become the guy she always wanted to meet.

So how about some of those objections you have? Here's the real truth behind them:

She's a good girl and would never put out on the first date:

Every girl is a good girl, and every girl will put out on the first date if she thinks you're the right guy and your timing is right. Don't worry about this issue. There's a time when it is best to pick a cherry from a tree. If you pick too soon, then the cherry is not good. Pick too late and, again it's not good. The next chapter will show you when and which cherries to pick, and then I'll show you how to handle them with care.

She's not that type of woman

Every woman is that type. You may not be having sex with her, but I bet you someone else is. On several occasions I've heard a buddy at work say about another employee, "she's not that type," when I'd been secretly doing the same girl for weeks or months. Every girl is that type of girl and every girl enjoys sex, but you have to be the guy who's confident, and sometimes discreet enough, to allow her to express her sexual nature.

She's married, or she has a boyfriend.

Women are always in relationships. They live for relationships. Most women feel naked if they aren't in a relationship. Many times you'll meet a girl, take her home, and have sex with her only to find out she's married. The point is, I've done many married girls or girls that have a boyfriend. This is usually not an obstacle for women. However, it's often an obstacle for men. Many men assume she's in *lock down* because she's in a relationship. This is a false assumption. Many guys also feel like they're breaking up a happy home. That's ridiculous! She's an adult and is making the adult choice to be with you as a lover. Her relationship is her responsibility, not yours.

While they're involved with someone, women often try to fulfill needs that aren't being met in their current relationship. By having sex with them, you're helping them fulfill these needs. You're doing her a favor! By following the System, you'll learn not to worry about whether or not the woman is in a relationship. She'll let you know if she wants to have sex with you. And if you can assure her that you'll be discreet, then the only decision factor is whether or not the encounter is worth the effort.

The bottom line is that someone

is doing her. If she meets the

profile and you follow the

System, you can be that

someone.

She's too hot. She could never want me.

Look around and you'll notice a strange thing. It isn't the most handsome men who have the most beautiful girls. I'm sure you've seen this often enough. You may think the guy has a lot of money or a huge cock, but that isn't necessarily true. Often, the reality is that the guy has skill. He knows how to excite her and how to keep her excited. He knows how to make her feel beautiful and sexy. He brings excitement into her life. He's a sweet challenge for her. You'll learn how to acquire this skill in future chapters. The bottom line is that someone is doing her. If she meets the profile and you follow the System, you can be that someone.

I'm not buff enough or rich enough.

Muscles and money do not get you sex. They may get you a better selection of women, but you also need skills. Think of it this way. There are many highly paid professionals who make six figures or above and never get laid. What money does for you is get the attention of a better quality of women. Women do like wealth, but if they give you all the signals and you don't know the steps to close the deal, then the woman you're after will go home with the guy who barely has enough cash to pay his rent.

Muscle is another powerful thing. Women love men with beautiful bodies. But likewise, I know many guys who spend hours working out, but never get laid. You can see these guys in the clubs every weekend. Their moves are amateur, or immature at best. Girls will spend the entire night checking these men out, but the guys always find some way to screw up the deal. The System shows you how to avoid these mistakes.

So, it's true that wealth and muscles makes initiating first contact easier most of the time. But even wealthy guys or guys with big muscles need to have techniques to get the women of their choice. Again, this book is not about buying sex or getting lucky. This is about a System any guy can use to always get laid, anytime. Read on.

If I had sex with her I would be using her or taking advantage of her.

This is a very damaging thought process for men. By having sex with women you are giving them the opportunity to get to know you. You are enriching their day and allowing them to have a good time with a great guy, instead of being frustrated with some wimp guy who's afraid to have sex with them. Plus, women love sex.

The important point is—you should be a good lover. No woman will complain about being used if she's having multiple orgasms each time you get together with her. Think of the options she has. Most guys are terrible lovers. I'm always amazed when I speak with my female friends to find out that they've never had an orgasm. As a man you should be confident, passionate, and a great lover to the women you take home. By doing this you're enriching her life, not using her. You are breaking her out of her boring life. You're doing her a favor. You're giving her experiences she will always remember with a smile.

We're friends and she doesn't think of me like that.

If she's your friend, she's probably already attracted to you. If you're a good friend, who will understand her needs better than you? As a true friend, you owe it to her. Do her, but do her well. The easiest panties to come off belong to girls who are already comfortable with you. They share their stories and their sadness. They share their happiness and their joy. They're emotionally attached to you. They probably secretly want you and fantasize about having sex with you. They may have been giving you the signals for weeks, months, or years now, but you hadn't yet acquired your skills. Your female friend has probably been frustrated trying to do everything possible to get you in bed, but you've been hung up on some friendship issues. She's not! If you're close friends with a girl it's most likely because she's already attracted to you. If you haven't had sex with her she probably thinks you're a pussy, a wimp, a nice guy. She doesn't respect you as a man or she would have already had sex with you. Wake up and smell the sex. Stop thinking about it and go do what you've wanted to do the entire time you've known her. Be a man and give her what she's been waiting for.

She's a friend of the family and would not be interested.

The friend of the family already knows everything about you she wants to know. You probably go to the same parties, the same church, and hang out at the same bars. It really doesn't get any easier than this. You've already established an immense comfort level with her.

Review the steps of the System and you'll realize that you're more than half way to taking off those panties.

My cock isn't big enough.

Some guys have big cocks and some have little cocks. Some girls have big tits and some girls have little tits. That's normal. However, when you're working her, she has no idea about the size of your cock, and it's irrelevant except in your head.

She's black or white or Asian or Latin or whatever, and I'm from a different culture, so she would never be interested.

Opposites attract. You can have sex with women from multiple cultures all over the world. But you have to know how to spot them. It's good to change flavors now and then to keep it interesting. Likewise, women like trying new things. It's like experimenting with new clothes. The very thing about you that's different may be the thing that she finds attractive about you. The 1% rule, discussed later, will explain in significant detail why you can have sex with girls from any culture or nationality without a problem. It's not about what makes you different from her, it's about how to spot the ones who are interested in you and how to follow the process of closing the deal.

The bottom line is that a big challenge for many men in getting laid is the way they think. To get past this, you must first explore your limiting beliefs about sex, having sex, and women. Once you identify these beliefs, ask yourself if they're beliefs based on fact or fiction. Where did you learn this information? Who told you this? Then challenge the beliefs. You may be surprised to learn that women love sex as much, or more, than you do. Once you challenge these beliefs you'll be surprised to find out just how many women are waiting on the sidelines for an opportunity to get into your pants.

The Top Reasons Girls Sleep with Guys

It's difficult to talk about confidence without identifying the primary reasons women drop their panties. So here they are:

Skill (game): There's no substitute for game!
You may have all the muscles in the world and
all the cash you need, but still have problems
getting laid regularly. We all know the guy who
seems to have everything – wealth, looks, body,
but can't seem to get a girl. If you don't have a
choice of girls whenever you want sex, then you
need to acquire skill.

So what is skill? Skill is being able to walk
into a bar with 100 girls, pick the one who's hot
for you, and leave together within minutes of
meeting her. Skill is being able to talk to a girl
in such a way that her panties are wet and her
heart is thumping as she does everything to try
and convince *you* to take her home. Skill is to
be able to toy with a girl, knowing that you can
close at any minute, knowing you have all the
choice and the control in the situation. Skill is
picking up a girl without being able to speak the
same language. Skill is the ability to perform at
the same peak level every time, because you
know it has nothing to do with luck. Skill is
never having a day without sex, unless by
choice. Skill is being able to find sex anywhere,
anytime. Someone once said that 10% of the
guys do 80% of the girls. Skill is being in that
10%, or better yet, to be in that 1% who have
sex with multiple girls at the same time,

whenever you want. Skill is what every guy needs to acquire so you'll never again have to rely on luck or be afraid of rejection. Skill is the focus of this book.

Fame: Fame is the only factor where you don't need skill to get laid. Just being recognized as a famous person will get you laid. But even famous people need to have some skill to help close the deal. Fame is difficult to acquire, and less than 1% of men in our society have it. The other 99% needs to rely on skill. Fame is amazingly good when it comes to getting laid. In fact, fame is better than wealth. You can be poor and famous and women will have sex with you just to have the bragging rights that they slept with a famous person. In fact, famous people often make a concerted effort to not get laid. They are in relationships and are often trying to avoid the girl waiting in the hallway with her panties in her hands. Or the girls in the front row flashing their breasts. If you're famous, there's a great chance you don't need what I have to teach. But if you're famous and you know what's in the pages of this book, you become a very dangerous man. Your greatest challenge may be whether you can close within 5 minutes or 60 seconds.

Wealth: Unless you're paying for sex, wealthy guys don't often get more sex than the average guy. Wealthy men are easy targets for women who want to use them. But closing the deal without using cash, gifts, or favors is just as hard for them as for the next guy. The difference between wealthy guys and other men is the quality of girls they can get, not the quantity of girls. Some wealthy guys are famous and will benefit from that fame (as described above). Most wealthy guys, however, are only known within a small circle. The hottest girls within that circle will usually make themselves available to the wealthy man. These guys can afford to have and keep the sexiest and highest quality women around. However, most of these men have fewer social skills than the average nerd. These people normally get their sex from others who set them up, or from women in their small circle.

Wealthy men will benefit from this book by learning how to combine their wealth with skills, resulting in more sexual closures than they ever imagined. Having wealth is one thing. Knowing how to use wealth to attract and keep sexy women is a separate challenge.

One of the main reasons

why wealth doesn't help a lot is that if you're in a club or in the supermarket, no one knows that you have a Porsche parked outside. No one knows you own the big house on the hill, and since many young women don't read financial magazines no one knows you were on the cover of Fortune a few months ago. And if you try to tell this to a girl while you're picking her up, you may come across as conceited. Some girls will buy that line, but many will be turned off unless the information is presented well. So having some game will certainly help someone who has a lot of money.

Wealth therefore is mostly useless, unless the girl *knows or believes* you're wealthy. There are several ways this can happen. One of the best techniques I've seen is from a single friend who has a large and beautiful home, and throws a party maybe three or four time per year, usually as the seasons change. He invites friends and makes it clear they have to bring female friends. At the party, he's the host. He has a contact sheet everyone signs in order to get invited to future parties. He never has to leave his house to get laid. He's an overweight and unattractive man, but women seem to ignore that fact once they see his house. He works the crowd during the party. He has a captive audience. Every woman can imagine living in that big, beautiful home. At the end of the party at least one or two women always stay behind. He works the contact list the following weeks and months, inviting the young and the beautiful back to the house for drinks, dinner, etc. He always gets laid and always shows up with a hot young girl every time I see him. He's got game! This is one way to use your wealth.

Muscles: I recommend every guy go to the closest gym today and start working out. Reason #1: girls can't help staring at a guy who has muscles. Reason #2: most guys are skinny, fat, badly shaped. Having some muscles gives you a leg up on the competition. Not having muscles does not prevent you from getting laid, but it will make it significantly easier to score if you do have muscles. Muscles sell! It's like girls with big tits. It isn't that guys don't like girls with small tits, but we simply can't ignore a girl with big ones. It's the same for girls when they're around guys with big muscles. Even if the guy is butt ugly, the girl won't be able to stop staring at him. She'll feel an uncontrollable urge to touch those muscles.

The first time this became undeniable was a few years ago in a bar where I was hanging out with some friend to have a few drinks after work. We'd popped into the local watering hole to drink beer and to try to "get lucky." One of the waiters looked as though he lived in the gym. The guy had a massive build with huge arms and chest. He had a tray in his hands as he made his way through the bar. Every woman in the bar stopped to let him through and some tried to touch his muscles. Others just stared and pointed to their girlfriend at the phenomenon that was in front of them. That guy could have done multiple chicks in the bar. He spent the whole evening turning down the girls we were all trying to get.

I had not yet developed the System, nor did I fully understand the true implications of what I'd just seen. But I signed up for the gym the next day and have never regretted it. Women love muscles as much as men love breasts. The more the better!

Looks (the handsome guy). The most handsome guys don't get laid any easier than other guys. That's partly because handsome is defined differently by everyone. It's difficult to get the same response from a woman regarding what constitutes a handsome or good-looking guy. So for the sake of discussion we define a handsome man as one who looks presentable, smells good, takes care of himself, and dresses well. This is a good thing, because women like a well-dressed man. Most guys fall into this category when they go out, so you gain no real advantage. But you are at a disadvantage if you don't meet the minimum standards for looks, dress, and hygiene.

The advantage comes from being a good-looking guy with game to back it up. If you look good and have no game, girls will think of you as a momma's boy or they'll wonder if you're gay.

Remember: The goal of the System is to be able to meet a girl, seduce her, take her home, and have sex with her within minutes of meeting her.

Chapter 3
Scoping

<u>**SCOPING**</u>
- Scan target area
- Identify target
- Confirm target

In a room of 100 people, how can you identify with confidence the one girl who will have sex with you that very night?

Scoping is Step 2 of the 5 Steps to Success. At this point I assume you've decided to get laid and have already challenged some of the limiting thoughts that affect your confidence. This is where we start taking action toward the final goal. Remember: *the goal of the System is to be able to meet a girl, seduce her, take her home, and have sex with her within minutes of meeting her.*

Now that I'm sure we're on the same page, we'll discuss Scoping. Scoping is the ability to find that needle in a haystack—the girl who will have sex with you TODAY. She's always out there, and the challenge is to identify her. There are other girls who might distract you from this goal. These are girls who enjoy receiving attention but aren't willing to give anything in return. Scoping shows you how to tell the difference. The distinction is small, but the results are large.

Imagine talking to 99 girls in a room only to find out the one girl you didn't meet was the one who wanted to go home with you? How could you know the difference? I see this all the times in clubs, bars, and everyday life. Guys are drawn to a hot-looking girl who's being an attention flirt. She toys with him, and then quietly leaves the club with her girlfriend, never to be heard from again. Later in this chapter we'll talk about how you can make the distinction between girls who just want to lead you on and the ones you really want to meet.

Scoping helps you identify the real deal, to see what other guys don't notice. It helps you avoid girls who are simply trying to get an ego boost at your expense. Scoping is the link between what you want and what she wants. She's already made the decision, but unless you can find her, she may have to go home alone and disappointed—again.

Whenever I think of scoping I remember this story: I went hiking in the Colorado Rocky Mountains with some friends a few years ago. As we were walking through the vast mountains a friend who was with us said, "Stop!" in a commanding voice.   We stopped. He said, "Do you see her?"

"What are you talking about?" I asked.

"The deer, over there," he said, pointing toward the woods ahead of us.

We squinted our eyes and followed his pointing finger, but I still saw nothing.

He said, "Look for movement, not the deer."

It still took some looking before we finally saw the buck standing a few hundred yards away, camouflaged among the brushes. My friend easily spotted the deer because he was a deer hunter. He'd had been trained to see deer and other wild animals by his father since he was a boy. That deer was always there, but most of us didn't know how to see it. Now when I go to the mountains, I show the deer and other wild animals to those I'm with, because I learned the skill from my friend   Similarly, I'll teach you the skill of seeing what was always there before you: the girl who's begging to get laid.

Scoping takes into account some harsh, yet beautiful, realities. This is primarily what separates the guys who always get laid from those who hope to get lucky. The first concept is the 1% rule.

What's the 1% rule?

Think of the 1% rule, this way. It's unlikely every woman will want to have sex with you on any given day. Even the most famous or skillful guy could never get *every* woman in the club. This is logical because some women will be with their boyfriends or husbands, on their period, just out of surgery, just having had sex, or disinterested for other reasons. One reason is that many women will simply not be attracted to you. It's not a bad thing; it's just a reality of life. Think of your own history. In the past you may have encountered girls who wanted to sleep with you, but you said "no" because you were in a relationship, you were on your way to an important event, or you just didn't find her attractive for some reason. So the first principle of the 1% rule is that no one can sleep with everyone at will. There are too many factors beyond our control.

The 1% rule is therefore based on the principle that at any moment 1% or more of the girls in your environment will be available to sleep with you within minutes of meeting them, and 99% (even though some may be interested), will not sleep with you immediately. This is a very critical and important concept, because some individuals may be able to attract 10% or 20% of the girls in the room, but will all of them say "yes" to today and now? Or will they simply say "yes" to giving you a phone number? This is not about getting phone numbers—this about getting laid within minutes of meeting the girl. It's important to keep that point in mind. *The 1% rule therefore states that at any given moment, in any environment, 1% of the women will be available for immediate sex with you.*

This is a statistically correct number. How many girls are at the beach on a given day? What does that 1% calculate to? How many girls would you have to choose from? How about the local bar or club? How about the center of town or the mall? But let's stick with the concept right now.   By accepting this fact, the question is not "Will I get lucky today". The question changes to "How do I identify, seduce, and take these girls home"

The true skill of always getting laid is the ability to identify the girls in that 1% category and to simply invite them back home. As easy as this is, most guys don't know how to do it. Most guys chase the 99% who are not immediately available and end up frustrated at the end of the evening as the girl says "goodnight" and disappears.

Let's be clear about the girls we're talking about. Every girl is a good girl and every girl will put out within minutes or hours of meeting her, given the right conditions. I know that's hard to believe, but it's true. Let's not chase our tails looking for bad girls because every girl likes a good sexual adventure. Bad girls are simply good girls with bad boys. You just have to be the man who can help her express that side of her nature. But for the sake of our discussion, it's important to understand three categories of women. This understanding will save you countless hours of frustration, painful rejections, and fruitless nights.

The Three Categories of Girls

For simplification, the System defines three categories of girls: Type "A," Type "B," and Distractions. These categories are used to simplify what is often a complex challenge for men. The challenge is simply, how does a guy know which girl will have sex with him? Or when will this girl have sex with him? These categories get straight to the point. Don't confuse them with girls you want to have long-term relationships with. This concerns only the girls you can get into bed within a short time period.

Type "A" Girls: These are the 1% you need to identify. They are the most critical to single men and they're out there waiting for you. These women will have sex with you within minutes of meeting them. They aren't bad girls; they're girls who are open to sleeping with you right away. It might be due to chemistry, adventure, attraction, holiday sex, a moment of weakness, or a hundred other reasons. The reason is not as important as the fact that these women represent 1% of those that you see every day. Follow the *5 Steps to Success* outlined in this book to identify and take immediate advantage of this situation.

Type "B" Girls: These are the "dates." They're girls who won't sleep with you within 24 hours, but will sleep with you within a few dates. These girls are attracted to you, but they're the "close later" instead of the "close now." Once you identify a girl as Type "B," take her phone number and wish her a good night. Always make sure you have a pen or some other way of taking her contact info. If you're bored in a few days you can call her and invite her over for dinner. The best time to do this is during the week. Most girls have nothing to do during the week and find any invitation an improvement over their current situation. See later in this book how to have inexpensive, effective, closures on dates.

Distractions: These are the majority of the women you'll meet. They are a big part of the 99%. It's not that you can never have sex with them, but typically it isn't worth the effort. They are either not interested or they may exhibit interest simply to boost their egos. These are the girls in the club who are dancing sexy with their girlfriends to get your attention.

ROY VALENTINE

After you buy drinks for them and their five girlfriends, they tell you what a nice guy you are. If you're lucky you'll get a handshake or a kiss on the forehead before they head out the door, laughing among themselves. Sound familiar? I have a friend who's an expert at being surrounded by Distractions. He always invites a group of friends to the club. Girls always bring their girlfriends. He buys everyone drinks. The girls all have boyfriends, but know when to show up for free drinks. The girls show up together and they leave together. He's never had sex with any of these girls, but I often hear them tell him what a sweet guy he is.

Don't get me wrong now. I think being a nice guy is good. But that's not what we're trying to achieve here. I have female friends who are simply friends. We go out, sometimes I get the drinks, and sometimes they get the drinks. We talk, we chill out, and we have fun. But they don't try to milk me to pay their bar tab or entrance fee for the club. The Distractions are women who make themselves seem available but are not. They pretend to be available in order to get an ego boost or to have men spend money on them. These are the Distractions and they should be avoided.

There's a different "A" Girl

waiting for you daily, and

countless "B" Girls.

So what does all this have to do with scoping? It's simple: If you know what you're looking for you have a better chance of finding it. What you are looking for are the **"A" Girls.** If you determine a girl is *not* an "A" Girl, then you should identify whether she's a **"B" Girl**. If she's neither an "A" nor a "B" Girl, then she's a *Distraction.* It's that simple. Sometimes guys like to make things more complicated by adding a thousand conditions to this easy concept, but there are no additional conditions. She's an "A" Girl, a "B" Girl or a Distraction. Many guys spend their time focused on the Distractions, which is why they never get laid. There's a different "A" Girl waiting for you daily, and countless "B" Girls. Now that we know what we are looking for let's learn where and how to find these girls.

How to spot them

There are many different ways to spot girls and pick them up. In fact, many guys use at least some of the techniques taught in this book. The various methods used materialize in many ways. Here are some of the ways.

Telemarketers: These are the guys who use the same line with every girl in the club. They have a numbers game going. They believe if they ask every girl they meet to go home with them, one will eventually say "yes." They believe the only way to find their 1% is to first be rejected by the other 99%. As painful as this seems, I've actually seen guys make it work. They're like the telemarketers who call your home during dinner, hoping you'll listen to the end of their pitch. The sales pitch is so ingenuous that you don't even have the patience to listen to it. Girls feel the same way about this heavy-handed approach. The guy is just a nuisance to them. An occasional woman will be polite enough to listen to this telemarketer, but most will stop the guy in his tracks, which is the same as hanging up the phone on a telemarketer. Personally, I would have a hard time with that method because the thought of being personally rejected by 99 girls in order to get to that one girl doesn't seem like fun. What these guys figure after a few years of rejection is that it's easier to be married. They simply get worn out and marry the first decent chick that comes along.

Dancers: This is another common approach. These guys hang out at nightclubs every weekend and will dance the entire night with any girl who agrees to dance with them. This guy believes that impressing a woman on the dance floor will convince her to go home with him. Maybe at some time in the past this worked for him. He danced, she said "yes;" he was convinced he'd found the key. Typically, however, a girl dances with a guy simply because it's fun to dance, not because she wants to have sex with him. She will go home with him if he's able to create a comfort level with her and if he knows how to close the deal. However, dancing is often a way for the girl to bring more *attention to herself* so she can catch the eye of the guy she really wants to go home with. Once the girl has enough fun, she politely says goodnight to Mr. Dancer.

It's important to remember that dancing is not closing. In fact, the two have little to do with each other. You may have danced with a girl in the past and closed the deal, but dancing with countless others brought no success. Scientifically speaking, you should conclude that dancing was not the main factor involved. You did something else right that got her to say "yes."

Touchers: Touching a girl in public before scoring with her is one of the fastest ways to turn a girl off. I've performed experiments by having my research assistants touch girls in bars or clubs when we were certain they were ready to go home and have sex. The results were almost always the same. She lost interest. Why does this happen? It's very simple. By touching her, you communicate that you want her. She's won the battle without having to risk anything. (See the discussion below about The Girl Game for more details on this.)

The second reason a woman loses interest after being touched in public by a man she hasn't slept with is that she interprets it as a lack of respect or desperation on your part. In either case, you've just disqualified yourself from the game. Every guy has had this happen at some time or another. You're in the club. Everything's going well. She's touching your chest or grabbing your butt, you're doing the same to her. You know she's hot and ready to go. Maybe you've both been drinking. You're kissing, then she says goodnight and disappears with her girlfriend. You're in shock as you try to understand what happened. Maybe you try to convince her of the value of going home with you. The more you try, the more you're convinced that you've just wasted the entire night with that "bitch." I hate to say it, but it was your own fault. You'll learn how to avoid these disappointing situations on future hunts.

So what's the right approach? Well, this is so simple that when I first tell it to guys they refuse to believe me until they try it. First, the goal is to find that 1% woman, the "A" Girl. To find the 1% you have to ignore the other 99% who are a mixture of B-Girls and Distractions. Here's the way this works. Women are always on the lookout for guys. They have fast eyes and process information at lightening speed. Most of the times a girl checks you out you probably won't notice. Why? Because you're a guy and you're waiting for Friday night or Saturday night to go the club and chase the 99% of girls that don't want you. Or worse, you're a guy who avoids eye contact or looks at the floor as you walk.

Guys like to go to clubs to chase girls because all the girls look totally hot on the weekends. This is, in fact, the worst place and time to meet girls. Remember what I just said: women are *always* on the lookout for guys. It's a fun game they play. If they can get the guy to look back, they score a point.

Guys are oblivious to this little game the girls play. This is why guys get confused about what is meant when a girl goes out with her girlfriend to have a "good time" or "have fun."

To go out and have fun for a guy often means drinking and getting laid. For girls, it does not. If a guy goes out with his friends, picking up a girl and taking her home is a major bragging right. Guys are proud of this and look forward to the opportunity to do it. We brag about it for years to come.

For girls it's different. If a girl goes out alone she is significantly more open to going home with a guy that she just met than if she were not alone. No one is there to see, no one will judge, and women typically really hate being alone.

If she goes out with one other girl, the girl is typically a good friend, a confidante, a roommate, or even a sister. They probably already have secrets between them and her friend would probably not judge her harshly if she were to leave and go home with a guy she just met, as long as the friend "approves" of the guy. The challenge in this situation is to create a comfort level and trust with both women.

If a girl goes out with multiple girlfriends, however, the situation is typically, at best, a "B" Girl situation. They are *not* out to get laid. In fact it is the opposite. To take home one girl from the group will prove to be extensively difficult to impossible. Their goal is to flirt, tease, get attention and show to the other girls that they can get the hottest guy to come on to them. They will take his number and flaunt him in front of the other friends but they will NOT go home with him that night. If they did, they would be judged very harshly as a whore by the other girls. They will dance with each other seductively, flaunt their sexuality and watch men drool. The girls are out to "have fun" and they are simply playing the *Girl Game*.

The Girl Game

Girls like to have fun! It true. They are always laughing, flirting, touching, and showing skin. This drives guys crazy, and girls know it. These are the skills girls have perfected to attract men. Girls are terrible in conversation with men. But they don't need to be good at that skill because they know a guy is interested before the guy actually says "hello." Sometimes they are not quite sure, so they continue to play until they are sure. This happens because women are very self-conscious about their looks and their ability to attract men. They have a constant need to know they can attract hot guys, similar to the way men feel about attracting hot girls. Each time a girl can confirm a guy is hot for her, it helps her confidence and boosts her ego. She doesn't have to sleep with the guy to feel successful. All she has to do is to be certain the guy wants to sleep with her. That's the Girl Game.

Why is this important to understand? It's important because in the dating game, this is the source of a woman's power. She will spend hours in front of the mirror to look good enough before going out. She needs to know she has the power to attract and seduce the guy she wants. Women like nightclubs because they feel powerful in these environments. They look hot and they know it. Guys are horny and will go after anything. Even the ugly girls get hit on. Since we're guys, here's a simple point system and scoreboard we can use to track points women get from each interaction they have with men in nightclub or other situations.

Activity	Point
She sees a guy check her out.	1
She sees a cute guy check her out.	2
The cute guy that she's checking out checks her out.	3
The cute guy that she likes asks her to dance.	4
She has confirmed that the guy wants her because he touched her.	5
Her friend's boyfriend is checking her out.	5

The more a woman can attract a man and know he wants her the more her ego goes through the roof. The more points she can rack up, the more *fun* she has. She doesn't need to sleep with anyone to go home with a healthy dose of confidence, since there are many willing participants to stroke her ego. The problem is, the more confidence she gains, the harder it is for a guy to score. Why? Because she doesn't have to negotiate anything. She already has what she came to the club for—an ego boost. So after checking her out (3 points), asking her to dance (4 points), and touching her ass (5 points), she now has 12 points of power over you. Why does she need you anymore? It was too easy for her. She'll just wait for a real challenge to come along.

So how can you beat her at her own game? Each time a guy approaches a girl and she sees that he's making a play for her, she racks up points. The more she gets a guy to respond to her, the more points she gets. What if she likes the guy, but he doesn't respond to her? Now she has a little challenge on her hands. She actually starts to lose points. What if she thinks he likes her, but he either doesn't respond or she can't confirm his feelings because he's toying with her? Then she starts to get a little obsessive. This is a true statement. The next chapter will show you how to pull the right strings until she starts to go crazy trying to identify if you like her. It's hard for her to walk away from this situation without getting her points.

Scoping, therefore, is the ability to identify the girl for the night *without* letting her know for sure if you're interested. There will need to be an element of uncertainty throughout the entire engagement until she's actually in bed with you. She will suspect, but you will need to play with that suspicion without confirming it until the last minute.

Scanning

Scoping therefore, contains two primary steps. The first is Scanning the second is Confirming. Scanning is a 24-hours-a-day, seven-days-a-week habit. Scanning can be done at the convenience store, the beach, a supermarket, church, or anywhere there are people. Wherever you have people, you have girls. Scanning is something girls do instinctively, all the time. Scanning is simply searching for eye contact. As you scan, you'll notice that many girls won't make eye contact with you. They aren't interested in you, and these are the girls you should not approach. Arguably, you can get girls to become interested in you, but why do the additional work? Why build a bridge when there's already one you can simply walk across? There are easy targets waiting to be discovered. Some have just broken up with a boyfriend and now have a free license to have sex with anyone they want to. Others may be in a relationship, but the sex is terrible and they're always looking to supplement the relationship with a sex stud on the side. Some are looking for the illusive Mr. Right. The reason they're looking is irrelevant. The fact is they *are* looking—and it's your job to find them. As you scan through your daily life you'll find about 1% of the girls you meet on a regular basis are ready, available and willing. These girls are at work, on the subway, in the restaurant—they are everywhere. It becomes a fun game because you never know where you'll find your 1% for the day. Keep looking and you'll know when you find her. *You'll know because she'll be looking back and she'll be scanning you, too.*

As you practice scanning, you'll find some places are better than others for you. This is your Market. This is the place that, for whatever reason, girls find you more attractive than other places. This could be a specific bar, or the mall, or the beach. It might be a place where you're well known, such as the local pub, work, or a place where your features are an asset, like the gym if you're well built. Whatever the case, the sooner you identify some specific markets, the more often you'll be able to get girls from these markets. Different places attract different types of girls. A jazz bar will attract a certain type of girl who will be attracted to a certain type of guy. If you're that kind of guy, then you may have found a good market for you.

The ideal target when scanning is a girl that is:

- By herself
- At any location
- At any time of day
- Giving you good eye contact

Confirming

As you scan and get eye contact you'll be able to better identify your target. Eye contact by itself does not mean much. It could simply mean you have something hanging from your nose or that she's simply scanning everyone else, as well. Therefore, you have to do one or more confirmation steps. This is simply an additional eye contact or two with the same person. The first eye contact could have been by chance, but a second or third eye contact is an invitation. She's working hard to let you know she's interested.

What if you don't get eye contact from the girl you want?

Let's assume that you're at the gas station and she's not looking your way. Or you're hanging out with your buddies and she's too busy being distracted by some event. What do you do? You simply move from where you're located, do a walk-by and pay attention to her reaction.

I always tell guys that

nightclubs are the worst places

to hunt for sex.

You may also simply get next to her or close to her and hang out. The intent is for her to get a chance to check you out to see if you're her taste for the day. If she's interested and you're watching the eyes, you'll be able to make eye contact with her. If you're sure she sees you and you did not make eye contact, then she's probably not interested in meeting you. Or, you may get an initial eye contact and she then avoids any further attempt to check you out. You were unable to complete the confirmation step. This is probably not an "A" Girl.

Does this mean that you would not be able to close on her? Not really, but it does mean that you would have to do more work than you would have to with an "A" Girl. If she's really hot and you MUST see if you have a chance, then go to the next step (see the following chapter) to do the introduction step. If she's still not interested you may be well advised to move on.

Nightclubs and other Hunting Spots

I always tell guys that nightclubs are the worst places to hunt for sex. It's true. I've hunted and scored at nightclubs because the System outlined in this book applies in any environment. A nightclub makes no difference. So why do I dislike hunting in nightclubs?

It's simple. Competition! Who needs it? I don't like competition any more than Microsoft likes competition, or General Motors likes competition. If your game is good enough you can always beat out the competition, but why make additional work for yourself. These are some of the primary things that are bad about hunting in nightclubs.

- By the time you've gotten there, a dozen guys have already approached her. Her points are through the roof. Even if she's hot for you she knows that she has tons of choices.
- She spent hours getting dressed. Again, she's feeling stellar. Her expectations are that she's so hot that the burden is on you to impress her. Again, who needs the work?
- She's probably with her girlfriends and playing the Girl Game. She may go home with you if she's only with one girlfriend, but girls are always afraid that her friends will think she's a whore if she goes home with a guy the first night they meet. So even if she's hot

for you she may automatically become a "B" Girl.

- The club is filled with the competition. Many of them have game, too. Or if not, they present a good distraction for her. Her ego is big enough to believe that she can have any of them.
- Girls tend to get drunk, throw up, and pass out. This takes the fun out of the sport. I usually pass on those opportunities. Leave those girls for the looser cleanup crew that has no game.
- Girls have an instinctive mistrust for guys they meet at a club. Their mothers and friends already warned them that these guys are out for one reason. Their mothers were right, but now you have to prove that you're not one of those guys.
- If you're wealthy, nightclubs work against you because you can't show off your assets. You're just like every other guy fishing in the pool of mud.

So if not nightclubs, where are good places to hunt, and why? Everywhere you go there are girls. It's simply true. Not only that, girls are a lot easier to take home if you meet them somewhere besides a club. The same hot chick that would barely give you the time of day in the club would be excited to meet you in the supermarket or on campus a few days later. The psychology of women is different when they're in a nightclub than during their normal lives. In nightclubs they are the hunted. They go to the club with their armor on and challenge you to crack through that armor. In their normal lives, however, they're just girls looking to meet a nice guy. That nice guy happens to be you—the wolf in sheep's clothing.

This is why hunting away from nightclubs work:

- Away from a hostile environment (the nightclub) their guard is down. They are more open to casual, non-threatening conversations.
- They didn't spend hours getting dressed to run to the supermarket and are actually surprised that you speak to them.
- Many girls get hit on only at clubs, which is why they like clubs—but that's also why they're suspicious.
- It's easier to connect when you can just talk with no distractions or loud background noise.

- Often when you meet a girl on the street, in the supermarket, at the department store etc., she lives only a few blocks away and is probably on her way home, anyway. She has nothing to do and wouldn't mind some company. The pickup becomes as simple as suggesting you walk her home or that she come home with you to hang out for a while. (See next chapters to learn how to do this.)

- Every girl has had a one-night stand from a club where the guy never calls again. Likewise, every girl fantasizes about meeting the guy in a normal situation where "our eyes just met and I knew he was the one." The story for her is significantly more romantic, and for you significantly easier.

Again, everywhere is a potential hunting spot, simply because everywhere you go you'll encounter women. Here are some ideas for different places: the beach (especially right before sunset), the mall (but not during large sales), community events (like local concerts and picnics), the local bar, the gas station, the grocery store, the department store, walking down the street (if you're walking in the same direction), at work, at church, at school, house parties, the video store, the library, on the airplane (captive audience), on the bus, on the train or subway, at tourist places (national monuments, tourist attractions etc.), amusement centers—anywhere. These are all places where women are vulnerable. Follow the steps and you simply can't miss.

Scoping Exercise

A good way to practice this step is to simply walk around looking into the faces and eyes of girls. Do this EVERYWHERE! Go to the mall where there are lots of girls and try to catch their eyes. Go to the beach and try to catch her eyes. At work, look dead into the eyes of that girl you've been hot for but afraid to ask out. Try to make eye contact with the girl you thought was hot for you. And do it with a little smile.

Make a mental note of each girl who maintains eye contact for a few seconds. After a few seconds look away. After another few seconds, look back at her with a smile. See her reaction. If she looks back and smiles or tries to hold back a smile, then you've got her. You've achieved Step #2 of the System. It's that easy!

This will become automatic after a while. You may be at the company picnic and the hot secretary locks eyes with you. Or you're walking down the street and some stranger with a beautiful rack is checking you out with a sly look on her face. Keep your eyes locked with hers for a few seconds. Look away, and then glance at her again with a smile. See her reaction. Practice this like a game everywhere you go.

This activity should always be *ON*. There should really be no *off* button. This might piss off an insecure girlfriend, so you may have to practice a little discretion, depending on your situation. I've made eye contact while driving on the highway, in church, on the train, in class, and while studying in the library. There's no limit to where and when you can use this technique.

To master this step of the System, many guys have to overcome a problem with looking at the floor. Many men are shy or form a habit of looking at the floor while they're walking. This is like throwing away obvious opportunities. You should never miss a pair of beautiful eyes. You may just miss the one who's waiting for you.

After doing this for a while, you'll know instinctively which ones are your 1% versus curiosity seekers. By following the System you will know how to close on these girls. Additionally, expect a very strange thing to happen. You will start noticing girls who are hot for you based on eye contact and you'll pass them up. Why would anyone want to pass up obvious sexual situations? You simply won't have time to have sex with all of them. Imagine if you get just one solid eye contact every two days. In a month, you'll have the opportunity for sex with 15 girls. Your closing ratio will increase, as you get better at this. After a few months you'll have a big problem with managing these opportunities. The girls you would do anything to get today will be the girls that you pass up tomorrow. But that's a good problem to have.

This is why the System is so powerful. Master each step and you'll learn that eye contact goes beyond language, culture, and country.

ROY VALENTINE

Of all the places I've visited

(over 20 countries), Japan was

the most challenging culturally.

Case Studies (Real-life Examples)

I put a great amount of effort into compiling this book to show and tell you how to get laid. I've included case studies to help illustrate how the System can be applied under various conditions—four success stories and two failures.

The stories are continued at the end of each chapter and are used to illustrate the points made in each chapter, showing how you can apply the process anywhere and anytime.

Case Studies (Eye Contact)
The Subway in Japan

I like this example because it shows the power of eye contact, followed up by the System. It's a powerful example because of the difficulty in breaking the Japanese cultural barrier. Of all the places I've visited (over 20 countries), Japan was the most challenging, culturally. The Japanese are not as open to Westerners as other Asian cultures and it's difficult for them to meet and speak to a total stranger. Additionally, they are culturally shy about making eye contact, and a woman will often look away if you are trying to make eye contact with her. This presented an interesting challenge! I'm proud to say, however, that the System didn't fail me and I had a great time there. I had many successes in Japan, but this one comes to mind more than others. It was my first Japanese experience.

I rode the subway to visit a city called Ginza, a popular shopping area in Tokyo, and then took the train on my way back to my apartment. The trains are clean and fast, and as a tall Westerner I stood out in the crowd. While leaving the train I made eye contact with a beautiful Japanese girl. I had completed the scanning step. I looked away and took a few steps down the stairs of the subway station. She was walking behind me as I looked back to do the confirmation step. Our eyes locked again and we both smiled. I slowed my steps as she caught up with me. She spoke no English and I spoke no Japanese. I realized immediately that I would have to be creative in following the remaining steps of the System.

On the Beach

I like to run on the beach. I do this for two reasons. The first is because I like to stay healthy. The second is because it's simply one of my best *markets* to hook up with girls. I actually had dark shades on that day, which is bad. Dark shades look cool, but they block eye contact opportunities. Remember that for eye contact to happen, both eyes must lock for a few seconds. Fortunately, my shades had slipped down my nose and I caught her eyes. She was alone on a towel a few steps in front of me. I looked to the ocean then back to her. I caught her eyes again with a smile. I'd just completed the second step and was ready to move on to the next step.

At the Bar

I like cruising bars. I like bars because there are usually several of them within a relatively small radius in most cities and they are usually free to get in. I also like bars because girls who come to bars alone are often looking to get laid. I also enjoy bars because groups of girls go to the club to mess with guys' minds, but they don't often go to bars together. It's strange but true. The above section of this book tells why I don't like nightclubs, so I won't go into that again. When I go to a bar I have a strict set of criteria. I don't like wasting time and am considered by many to be an efficiency nut. I guess developing an efficient system to pick up girls proves that point.

So here are some things I go by:

- If I don't see any women ALONE who are attractive, suitable candidates, I don't even enter the place.
- I usually walk from the front of the bar to the back, around, and then to the front again to scan the women.
- If I don't get an eye contact, I leave and move on to the next bar.
- If I get an eye contact I will only stay if she's alone or with one girlfriend. More than one girlfriend, I leave.

So here's the process. I find the "bar strip" in the area. I start at the first bar and look in. If single girls are present I walk through the bar from front to back, around, and back to the front, scanning. If I get a hit I hang around, maybe grab a beer, and move to the next step of the System. If I don't get a hit, I move to the next bar. You can efficiently work through a lot of bars this way. I stay only at the bar where I can fulfill this step of the System. If there's no eye contact then I am probably wasting my time. I don't need the extra labor. If there's a hot girl who's alone and I don't get an initial contact, I try to walk near enough to her to see if

I can get her attention via eye contact. If still nothing, then I move on. If I do get a hit though, then it's time to play the game.

Here's an example: I was on a business trip in a major USA city. I went to dinner and on my way back to the hotel I stopped at a couple of bars. I came up with nothing. Not one hit. I was tired, so I headed back to my hotel. I stopped at the hotel bar and saw a girl. She was actually with a group. This would normally disqualify her, but the signals were clear. The confirmation was screaming and she didn't seem to be with any particular person in the group. She left the group and headed to the rest room, her eyes locked on me the whole time. I decided to move to the next step of the System. I thought I'd give it a shot.

A "10" Hot Chick

Hot girls are harder to close on than the average girl, but the basic principles are the same. However, the execution is a little different in a couple of steps. This is an example of a girl who was a friend of a friend I partied with for a day.

It all started with eye contact. My friends had tried for months to close on her, but none of them knew of anyone she'd closed on.

She was a super hot 19-year-old blonde with a petite body. I imagine she never had a moment of peace without guys hitting on her.

We met. The eye contact was brief, but it was there. She had the bored look of a girl who's hot and knows it. I normally pass up on these girls because they usually aren't worth the effort. But my buddy challenged me, betting that I couldn't close on her. He had already tried and had failed miserably.

I accepted the challenge.

Amateur Hour – Another "10" Hot Chick (the Failure Story)

It takes a lot of failures to eventually create success, and I'm no different. This is a story of one of those failures. And yes, in the past, there were many.

I'm hanging out with my buddies. We're at the beach and see three hot chicks, all on the 7- to-10 scale when it came to looks. Of course, I had to go after the "10."

Amateur Hour – The Nightclub Story

By the time you're finished with this book you'll get a clear understanding that nightclubs are not the best places to pick up girls. Additionally, you should learn that most of the time you can't recover from bad game. It's important to realize the reason you're out hunting. If it just an opportunity to feel up tits and asses in a night club, then this is the wrong book to read. If the reason is to get laid, then you're at the right place. Here's an example of where I had my priorities wrong.

I went to hang out with a buddy of mine. This was awhile back when I still thought that picking up girls meant getting dressed nicely, going to the club, meeting a girl, telling her how hot she was, asking her to dance, grabbing all the ass I could get, doing some tongue kissing, and my God—I might get laid if I got lucky. After all, it makes perfect sense that if I can kiss her, play with tits, and get her really hot in the club (especially a dark club), then she would definitely come home with me. That's what amateurs believe and at one time I was no different.

So I went to a club with a buddy of mine. We hung out, had a few drinks, and each started our rounds of hitting on chicks. I spotted one hanging out with her girlfriends. She had a short skirt on with a very hot revealing top. I figured if she was dressed that hot, she must be looking to get laid. I'd been shot down a couple times already, but I figured she was worth a try. Plus, if I got lucky, man—that would be some nice stuff to get into.

I marched over and asked her to dance in front of her girlfriends. To my surprise, she said "yes".

Note: These stories continue throughout the book as examples of how the System can be applied. The examples walk through what to do and what not to do in these situations while applying the System.

ROY VALENTINE

Being able to identify the right

girl is practically a science.

What happens next is an art.

Chapter 4
Making Contact

<u>**MAKE CONTACT**</u>
- Proximity
- Introduction
- Confirm interest

In 60 seconds or less, how can you be sure she wants you?

Being able to identify the right girl is practically a science. What happens next is an art. The first thing to understand is that if eye contact is made, a girl expects the guy to come over and talk to her. This affirms her power and control over the situation. She likes when this happens and is flattered by it. This however, it's exactly what you should NOT do.

Remember the points system I mentioned in an earlier chapter? Your goal is to confuse her system and make *her* work for her points. If they come too easily, she will not appreciate what you have to offer. Women never respect a guy who falls at her feet with the first sign of her interest. He's too easy and is no challenge for her.

On the other hand, you do need to make contact. To accomplish this, you must establish proximity without giving yourself away. In other words, you need to get close to her without letting her think it was her magnetic power that achieved this result. There is a subtle but important point here that you must understand: If a guy makes eye contact with a girl across the room and walks directly up to her, he looses an advantage because she knows she has him. However, in the same situation, if the guy achieves proximity by waiting a minute or two and then making his way to the girl indirectly, she isn't sure if it was her power or some reason that brought him near her. Either way, if the interest is really there she will make herself available for the pursuit. The game has just begun.

For definition's sake, proximity is achieved when you are physically close to the girl. You're standing next to her where it's possible to have a conversation. You are within arm's length of her.

Here's how to accomplish this in a club or bar:

(1) Establish and confirm eye contact.
(2) Grab a beer or drink from the bar.
(3) Make your way next to her without a direct frontal approach.

In another environment:

(1) Establish and confirm eye contact.
(2) Walk by as though you're distracted by something else.
(3) Make your way next to her without a direct frontal approach.

If you're already next to her, perhaps if you're ordering a drink and she's sitting at the bar, proximity is already established. In this situation you would:

(1) Establish and confirm eye contact.
(2) Make an introduction (see below).

How to convince her to have sex with you

Many guys believe you have to convince a girl to have sex with you or trick her into the act. After all, girls don't want sex—only guys do. That's so wrong! You'll only have to convince a girl to have sex if she really doesn't want to have sex with you. That can be a lot of work. Imagine someone trying to sell you a car when you have no interest in the car or you don't have the money to buy one. Eventually, they might be successful, but wouldn't it be easier just to find someone who wants to and who can afford to buy that car? It's the same with girls and sex. You should never have to convince a girl to have sex. That makes you vulnerable and gives her an advantage and all the power in the conversation. It also opens you up for major rejection. The System teaches you how to identify the 1% of girls that already want to have sex with you. Sometimes the eye contact is so powerful and her body language is so clear that the other steps are simply a formality. You therefore don't have to convince her of anything or risk being rejected by her. You simply make her feel comfortable that she's making the right decision. The following steps show you how to accomplish this mission.

The Introduction

Before discussing introductions, I'll list some of the worst introductions a guy can make to a girl—things that will immediately disqualify you. You have to realize that if this girl is especially attractive she has guys hitting on her every time she leaves the house. Because of this, she has heard all the common and boring intros and lines. By using these old lines you're practically insulting the woman's intelligence. Plus, the System dictates that an introduction should not be a pass. An introduction should be a validation of interest. Here are some of the worst:

(1) ***Hi, my name is Bob (or Jim or whatever).***
Who cares what's your name? She won't remember it in a few minutes anyway. It's like saying "Hi, my name is boring and I'm pretty lame and would you please give me a shot at having sex with you?

(2) ***Don't I know you from somewhere?***
This is almost a line from a horror movie for many women. She knows she

doesn't know you and once that's established in the next five seconds, you have nowhere to carry the conversation.

(3) ***You're the most beautiful girl I've seen in my life (or the most beautiful in the club, or the most beautiful I've seen today etc.).***

You've just established her as superior to anything you can ever hope to get. You've just raised her ego beyond where it already was, which was probably pretty high, and confirmed that she can do much better than you tonight.

When guys use these lines they come across like used car salesmen. She already knows all you want is sex, so let's not confirm it. A girl is actually surprised, or intrigued, when she *thinks* a guy may *not* want her. She almost doesn't know what to do with herself. This builds a little intensity and challenge. But, we're not there yet. Let's get into good introductions.

A good introduction should have nothing to do with sex. In general, a good introduction should be spontaneous and relevant to the present situation. It should be open-ended and require a response. A good introduction gives the girl an opportunity to respond in a discussion format and not a one-word response. Here are some examples:

In a bar a comment could be made about the band. An example might be: "They're pretty good! Do they play here every week?"

Her response at this time is very important in your validation of her interest. If she's interested she will respond in a conversational way. "I don't know. This is the first time I've heard them play, but I really like them a lot." She'll probably respond with a smile and positive body language. (See below for body language signs.)

If she's not interested she will either ignore you or simply say "no," and give you her back, or simply focus her attention away from you. This is a good point at which to exit the scene, unless you want to do an additional verification question. If you do and the response is similar, it's time to move on and continue the search. Anything else would be harassment to the young lady. She may be someone else's 1%, but she is simply not yours. So let's not waste time. Your true 1% is still waiting to be discovered.

Assuming that the response was positive, it's time to do a follow-up question. Remember, *conversation is simply a string of questions and answers.* A follow up question might be: "Yeah, I've been trying to find a place that plays this type of music. Is this the only place in town that plays jazz (or whatever), or are there other places?"

Again if the response is friendly, then continue the conversation. It's important to watch the body language and listen to the words closely, especially in the first minute or two, but also throughout the entire conversation. A woman's body language will typically say if she's interested and display her level of interest much more than her words will. To ignore these signals can be disastrous. It's very easy to screw up a potential situation simply by not reading the signals she's sending. To help with this, I've listed some of the most common body language signs to watch for.

Women's Body Language

Eye Contact

We've discussed this one extensively, because it's extremely important. Eye contact is a reactive action that is achieved when someone interesting or different is seen. Eye contact that lasts a bit longer than normal or that is repetitive (she keep looking over at you) typically means some level of interest from her in you. Extended eye contact, especially in a conversation, is a definite green light. Walk through each step of the System as fast as you can and enjoy the fruits of your labor.

Playing with her hair

This is a nervous reaction that is exhibited by most women. This often happens in situations where she's interested in the guy but not confident he's interested in her. It's also a self-conscious form of grooming to check that she's looking good, hair in the right place, etc. This is a positive sign.

Touching the arm or chest of the guy

Women do this very expertly in the middle of a conversation. It's an openly flirtatious move. This is often done when she is interacting with a well built/muscular or physically attractive guy. She will do this to guys she wants to have sex with or guys she knows she can't have sex with but wants to feel his build. In other words, she's feeling him up but trying to seem innocent about it. Girls that are "just friends" do this a lot with guys to whom they're sexually attracted.

Looking past the guy or looking around
This is a bad sign. She's not interested and she's hoping to meet someone else. You may get lucky if she doesn't have any other options, but you're not the #1 choice of the moment. This often happens on the dance floor or during the conversation stage.

Looking at, looking away from you
This is the same as direct eye contact. She looks at you then looks away, a little embarrassed. She does that time and time again. She's interested or very interested, depending on which step in the System this happens. This can often be a good justification to make a close step. (See section on Close the Deal.)

Cross the arms
This is another bad sign. She's uncomfortable. You need to change the topic of conversation, become extremely funny, or find a way to relax her.

Playing with ear or earring
This is a good sign. She's feeling girly and self-conscious. She's curious about you or cares what you think about her. Watch for the

personal questions at this time like "So, do you have a girlfriend?"

She's stiff to your touch or your hug

You should probably run and not walk. She has no interest in you. Maybe she's been polite in the conversation, but you certainly have not achieved a comfort level with her. This happens often when a guy tries to close the deal without going through the prior steps. Rejection is imminent. At this point, work on creating a comfort level or simply find a polite way to excuse yourself from the scene.

She allows you to touch her arm

You've achieved some level of comfort with her. Continue with the steps to closure.

She squeezes your hand

Bingo! Notice the smile that follows her squeeze? She's definitely your 1%. Continue through the steps to closure.

Hugs and kisses

Hugs and kisses have no specific significance. The length of the hugs and kisses means a lot. The longer the hug or kiss the better your chances.

She brushes her hand against you or 'accidentally' brushes her breast against you- especially after speaking with you for a while.
Bingo! Again, notice the smile that follows her physical contact. Physical contact is usually not an accident by women. It's one of the most prominent sign of comfort with or attraction to you. She's definitely your 1%. Continue through the steps to closure.

Therefore, if the introduction was successful, including the follow-up question and a positive body language then you've successfully completed this step. It's now time to get connected.

Case Studies (Make Contact)
The Subway in Japan

After I confirmed eye contact, I realized this girl could be my potential 1%. Needless to say, I was very excited. She was like a cute Asian doll with a big smile, and there's nothing like doing a native. It's one of the pleasures of traveling. I slowed my step as I headed down the stairs of the subway station. I didn't want to be too obvious by stopping and waiting for her, which would have given her too many points. She caught up shortly and I made some comment about the subway station.

She had a puzzled look on her face. She smiled and responded in Japanese. I tried again, and received a similar response. I thought, "Oh, shit!" but the body language, the smile, the attitude were all clear. I couldn't walk away. We walked down the stairs, both trying with futile attempts to communicate. Verbal communications failed, but the body language still showed interest. I used my hand to direct her to follow me. She complied. We walked through the subway until we reached a little market.

On the Beach

I received my confirmation from the woman sitting on her towel. It was a steaming hot day and I was vacationing on a tropical island. The ocean was blue as it washed up to the shore with white suds. The beach was sprinkled with a mix of locals and tourists. There were coconut trees and bamboo huts where various types of alcohol were sold. I strode past my admirer and left her with a smile. I wanted her to wait and I didn't want to seem eager. I know the Girl Game and wanted her to work for her points.

I got a beer from a bamboo hut bar at the end of the white sandy beach. The bartender was a dark man with a big smile. We exchanged pleasantries before I headed back towards my end of the beach, making sure I walked closer to her.

"So what do you think of my beach?" I asked her.

"Your beach?" she replied.

"Yes, I wanted to know if you were having a good experience." She smiled and told me she'd arrived that day and that it was more beautiful than she imagined. The Caribbean is always a beautiful getaway.

At the Bar

The eye contact I got from her required me to make an attempt, so I needed to achieve proximity. I headed to a junk food machine between the restroom and her destination. It was near the restroom and she'd have to pass it on her way back to the table. I pretended to buy something from the machine, though I don't eat junk food.

When she left the restroom she seemed pleasantly surprised to see me struggling with the machine. Pretending to be clueless, I asked her if she knew how to use it. She said "yes" and volunteered to help. In a minute I had a Snickers bar after she figured out that my dollar bill was bent and needed to be straightened out. I thanked her and asked about the friends she was hanging out with. Turns out they were colleagues from work; it was someone's birthday and they were having a celebration. I asked her how late she'd be partying with them, since it was already about 10:00 pm. She said she was sure everything would be over soon, maybe less than half an hour.

A "10" Hot Chick

Before we went out I took a minute to speak with her privately. We had been drinking. We were to meet some other friends at a local nightclub later that night. In my conversation I made sure to apologize and to tell her that she shouldn't be offended if I didn't spend much time with her. She seemed like a nice girl, but she wasn't my type. I liked girls with a little more color and a little more ass than she had. If she liked, I could introduce her to a friend or someone else later in the evening.

I think she was a little surprised by this, but she was cool. I said it in a respectful and reassuring way, as though I were just trying to be considerate of her time. She was visiting and I wanted to make sure she had a good time.

We all went to the club. She was smoking hot! I was now just a buddy who didn't want to get into her pants and we could talk as friends. I talked to her on a couple of occasions while we walked from the car to the club and commented about a Latin girl and a black girl we walked by that were very hot. "Now that's what I like," I said to her with my eyes trailing the hot round butts of the passing girls.

I bought her a drink in the club. We were friends now. I watched as guys drooled and tried their best to get her attention. She was definitely one of the hottest girls in the club. I gave her no compliments, except something like "Yes, it's a nice outfit," with little to no conviction. I did not ask her to dance, although she kept coming over to hang out with me. I danced with other girls and she danced with other guys. It was a fun project. I was her confidante between dances. The entire group was having fun.

Amateur Hour – Another "10" Hot Chick (A Failure Story)

We walked over and started talking to them. They were hot and knew it. There were three girls and three guys. At first there didn't seem to be much interest on their part, but we worked the situation and they started to participate. The conversation was now pretty lively with a good exchange.

The girls were students and attended the local college, and all three had great career aspirations. My friends and I were all seasoned professionals and were willing to give free advise about the general business market. We were even willing to show them a good time if they wanted to go out sometime. I got the phone number of the one I was talking to, as did my friends.

Amateur Hour – The Nightclub Story

When I saw her with her friends, I just had to ask her to dance. She was hot and I hoped I would get a shot at her. When she said "yes" I was pleasantly surprised. We headed through the crowd to a good spot on the dance floor. The music was hip-hop. We were swinging our hips and having a great time.

It wasn't long before they were playing a booty-shaking song that gave me a great opportunity to grab her hips and pull her closer. She did nothing to stop me.

ROY VALENTINE

Our core concept is that it's possible to sleep with almost any woman within minutes of meeting her ...

Chapter 5
Establish Connection

ESTABLISH CONNECTION
- Achieve comfort level
- Achieve trust
- Confirm interest

What should you do to get the really hot girls?

Establishing connection is a critical part of the System. Our core concept is that it's possible to sleep with almost any woman within minutes of meeting her—if you can achieve a certain level of comfort or connection with her. Therefore, the goal of this step is to establish a connection with her and help her to achieve a comfort level with you.

How is it possible to achieve this goal? Furthermore, how is possible to achieve this goal within minutes of meeting her? This goal is now significantly easier because we've already accomplished the first steps. Once you've established and confirmed eye contact, proximity and a comfort level then sex with this girl is imminent. It will simply be a matter of time and closing technique. But first, let's talk about how to establish this connection and create a comfortable environment for her.

To establish connection with another human being is quite simple. You need only find a topic of interest for the person and give them the opportunity to talk about it. This is true of any two human beings, in both personal and business situations. The System acknowledges this as a core part of human interrelationships. During this step of the System it is important to establish things this person is interested in. To do this we continue from the last chapter where you had a successful introduction.

From that introduction you created an initial comfort level, curiosity, and some level of sexual interest via your initial eye contact.

The next step is to start asking the girl about herself. A mistake men often make here is to begin spouting information about their jobs, financial situations, problems, or issues. In reality, even though she may ask about these things or may be polite enough to suffer through minutes or hours of these details, she would prefer to talk about herself. *The #1 most interesting topic to a woman is herself.*

The main thing to remember about good conversation is that the more the other person talks, the more they feel they know you, and the more comfortable they feel with you. It also makes her feel connected to you. You can interject bits of information about yourself and your interests, but the conversation should clearly be about her and the things she finds interesting. General topics women like to talk about are their day, traveling, relationships, etc. What a guy should do at this point is to ask follow-up questions about the things the girl has already said. Also, it's important to summarize the things she just said occasionally so that she feels "heard." It's equally important to never try to "solve" her problems. If she's had a bad day, she doesn't want you to fix it, she simple want to express it. She wants to feel "heard." For instance:

Guy: So you like to travel? Where have you been?

Girl: Well, I spent some time this summer in the Caribbean. I went to Jamaica and the Cayman Islands on a cruise ship and we stopped at a few other ports.

Guy: Really, at which other ports did you stop?

Girl: We went to the Bahamas as well, from the Port of Miami.

Guy: So you went to Jamaica, Cayman and Miami? What did you do there? Is it true everyone parties like crazy there?

Girl: Well, blah, blah, blah....

Guy: Or really? Blah, blah, blah... How about blah, blah, blah...

Get my point? It doesn't matter what the topic is. What's important is that she gets an opportunity to talk about it and you show interest by listening, summarizing, and asking more questions.

So how long do you have to listen to this? It's possible to keep a conversation going like that for hours. Each time you summarize what she said, she feels you're the greatest listener and you really understand her and care about her. You don't just want sex like all the other guys; you're really interested in HER. This creates the connection and trust required to close the deal.

Another way to keep her talking is the affirmation technique. As tempted as you may be to jump in and tell your story, don't. In fact a part of flirting is to *say as little about yourself as possible*. The point here is to keep her curiosity high about you and to keep the attention on her. This is her greatest need. It always is! All that is required to affirm what she says is an occasional comment, such as: "Really?"… "No way!"… "Did she actually say that to you?"… "Wow!"… "That's incredible!" She can talk for days like this. Here's an example:

Girl: So we were on the boat and this couple just started to make out in the pool
Guy: Really!
Girl: Yes, it was like they were going to have sex right there.
Guy: No way!
Girl: And he actually started taking her top off while everyone was watching.

Guy: No way, you got to be kidding!
Girl: My girlfriend couldn't believe it. Blah, blah, blah…

Again, this could continue forever with affirmations and a new question thrown in now and then to keep it interesting. Also. keep your affirmations tone excited and even with a high pitch. Sound surprised, interested and excited. Be animated with your facial expression and your voice. She'll think you are a great listener.

Flirtation

During this conversation it's important to hint towards your interest without actually proclaiming it. One of the quickest turn offs for a girl is knowing for a fact that the guy wants her. One of the best turn-ons for a girl is thinking the guy may want her, but not knowing it for sure. Her curiosity will tempt her into going quite a distance to finding out for certain what his intensions are. It is this weakness that flirtation exploits.

Flirtation includes eye contact, but not staring. Staring at a girl confirms you really want her. Once this confirmation has been established, she will most likely move on to more challenging subjects. Winking at a girl or whistling does the same thing. However, a quick look and then looking away, maybe with a smile, creates curiosity and intrigue. This is why the introduction, then the conversation, must enhance that intrigue and build intensity. Anything that's too easy is lessened in value. Therefore, *a core component of successful flirtation is to appear slightly unavailable or uninterested, but not unattainable.*

There's a fine line here. If you appear too uninterested, you may loose the other person's interest. But if you seem too available, you reduce your own value. The middle ground is to do both, thereby confusing the girl. Let her work for clarification.

How is this done? Well, flirtation is all about confusion. You do something, and then you do the opposite. You're available, but you may not be available to her. You're interested, but you're not sure. You're confident, but you may not want her. You're interested, but distant. She will desperately try to get clarification. The excitement of her curiosity will lead her from the bar or the mall to your home. **She must never resolve this confusion or have this curiosity satisfied until she is back with you in your home where you make the** *final move*. It is not until her panties are off that she will really get it. She's been played. This is especially important for really hot girls. They can sense your interest but cannot control the curiosity. She will have found the entire experience exciting and exhilarating.

The intensity of flirtation is built up via a combination of body language, words, and tone of the voice. It's the hook needed to reel the fish into shore. Maybe a look that shows physical interest followed by a verbal statement that she's not your type, followed by staring at another woman who could be your type. It's the center of the game. Eye contact was established, connection and comfort level are established, now she's confused because she's not sure if you want her. That makes you an interesting species.

As you carry out this flirtation, your voice should shift from serious to playful. Your body language must be confident. Push your chest out whether standing or sitting. Shift from a sly smile to a smug look at will. She'll be reading every move in her effort to calculate your intent or next move. Her desperation to satisfy this curiosity will make her available to various types of suggestions. She'll find it all exciting and will be surprised at herself in the morning. Nothing will stop her from biting the hook. In the morning, don't be surprised if she says, "I can't believe I did that" or some variation of that comment. She won't be lying. She really just couldn't help herself.

How to flirt with really beautiful girls

Again, another word for flirtation is confusion. Really beautiful girls, the "10's" of this world, flirt even more than anyone else. They use their beauty, charm, and the promise of premium sex to confuse and cloud the minds of men everywhere. They simply don't need to put out as much as other girls do. This is because they always have boyfriends who spend time kissing their asses, and they cannot leave the house without hearing a dozen guys say how hot they are. In other words, they understand that men will do anything to get into their panties and they know they have total control of these men.

But that level of confidence is also their greatest weakness. They're banking on the idea that any guy they want, they can have. But what if a really beautiful girl is even slightly attracted to a guy and he rejects her? This is devastating to a girl like this. Her ego is shattered. Remember the points system? A rejection like this actually takes away points from anyone. It's more dramatic for her, however, because she's not used to having that experience. She has always been in control of men and their interaction with her, but now she's not. She's confused. There must be something wrong. He must not realize what he's passing up. What's wrong with him? This becomes a challenge. To what extent would she go to prove she can have him if she wants to? So here's an example of how you would flirt with a girl like this.

    (1) Eye contact was established and
         confirmed (same as before).
    (2) Introduction was successful.
    (3) Conversation is friendly.

The conversation at some point will get to interests.

Girl: So what type of girl do you like?
Guy: Well, it depends!
Girl: Depends on what?
Guy: Well, I don't want you to take this personally. I mean, you're OK, but I'm

normally not into blondes (*or whatever characteristics describe her*).

Girl: (*Most likely with a frown*) What do you have against blondes? I'm a blonde. (*Even if she wasn't really interested a minute ago, now you've peaked her curiosity and interest.*)

Guy: Well yes, you may be different but I like smart and ambitious girls. (*Nonchalantly*)

Girl: (*She's probably a little irritated here and may want to use the word asshole to describe you, but she's also challenged. She has been hit off the pedestal and needs to regain her title of "princess".*) Hey, I have a degree in business and I'm Account Manger at XYZ Corp. (*She's now on the run and trying to prove her value.*)

Guy: Well, I'm sure you're OK but I've always found brunettes are not only smarter but also a lot more fun. (*The setup.*)

Girl: So I'm not smart or fun because I'm a blonde?

Guy: It's not like that. I mean (*innocent, devilish smile*) I like girls I can take hiking, who have no problems having sex in the woods or on the beach without being worried about breaking their nails.

Girl: Hey, I love camping. And you'd be surprised what I like to do in the woods. (*She pretty much did the close for you.*)

Guy: So do you really believe you have what it takes to keep my interest? (*Game over.*)

Notice the conversation changed to her defending herself and trying to be good enough to meet *your* standards instead of you trying to meet her standards. This position should be maintained flirtatiously for the entire time up until she's in bed with you. She should never get the thumbs-up that she's good enough until after you've had sex with her. She needs to prove she's as good as the other girls that you find attractive. If she gets you to sleep with her, she will feel a sense of conquest she hasn't felt before. Make no attempt to let her think you really want her. In fact, you may even point out other girls who are more your type. Tease her about why you would hesitate before taking home *a girl like her*. However, do this in a confident way. For instance, let her know that you have choices in the women you take home. Don't say something like, "You remind me of my ex-wife." We're not going for the pity move here, we're going for the confidence move. Most hot girls are too self-absorbed to do the *pity fuck* thing. They all want to conquer the big wild bull that can have anyone he wants. Here's a sample conversation of this technique:

Girl: So what do you mean you wouldn't date a girl like me?

Guy: Well, don't take it personally, but I just met you. You could be some psycho-chick

Girl: I can't believe you just said that.

Guy: Well, you never know. Plus listen, you're kinda cute, but so are a lot of girls here.

Girl: But I'm not like the other girls.

Guy: I know you're not, but it's not like it's a big challenge to get laid around here. *(Every girl secretly thinks all the other girls are whores and that guys can get sex whenever they want.)* What makes you different? Are you some kind of super lover or something?

Girl: Well, I've never had any complaints.

Guy: Really, what does that mean?

Girl: I bet you'd like to find out. *(slyly)*

Guy: Not really. It doesn't matter. But we're here talking. If you want to confess to something, go ahead.

Notice the sparring and the subtle slams by the guy. Notice the defensive tones from the girl. This is actually a good thing. It can be a delicate line, but a necessary one, because many hot girls believe themselves to be God's gift to men. The guy in the conversation is saying,

... when it is challenged,

especially by a man they are

interested in, they find the

challenge intoxicating.

"Hey, you're not bad, but I'm not desperate. Show me what you've got." Hot women can't resist that type of confidence. Remember the majority of interactions these girls have with men is simply a repeat performance of the ones they've have had since they were little girls. They learned very young that being a pretty little princess gives them any boy or man they come across. They learn they can be a total bitch and the man is still happy just being in their presence and that the bitchier they are the more attention they get. This assumption is rarely challenged. However when it is challenged, especially by a man they are interested in, they find the challenge intoxicating. They fall prey to their own game.

If you're not confident enough to challenge a girl like this, just remember that she only knows about you what you tell her. Therefore, don't ever say, "You intimidate me" or "You are the most beautiful girl I've seen in my life" or "I can't believe I'm here talking with you". Those are clear signs of lack of confidence. In fact, the less you say about yourself, the better off you'll be.

If you're really shy, maybe you can think of a character you'd like to be to help with your confidence. You can be the rich producer who's scouting for talent, who might consider her for a small role in your next movie. Or the talented writer who would like to interview her privately for an upcoming book. Or you might be a rich, successful entrepreneur who's not sure if she's worthy of your time. How about a well-traveled photographer with a wealth of photos she must see? Use the same character on different occasions until you're comfortable and confident in that role. Also, don't say much about your character, just hint casually during the conversation. Her curiosity will force her to ask various questions, but pretend to be private or guarded while confirming only the facts you want her to know. She cannot possibly verify the facts before you get her to bed. Sometimes the mask of another personality gives a guy the confidence of a superhero. And if she's shallow enough to sleep with you only because she thinks you're wealthy or famous, then she has only fallen into her own trap. Here's a sample dialogue:

Guy: Well, I'm in the entertainment business.
Girl: Oh, you're an actor
Guy: Is it really important? I really would prefer to get to know you better.

Girl: It's not a big deal, but why are you so secretive?

Guy: I'm not trying to be secretive. I just don't want girls to like me for my wealth.

Girl: I know some girls are like that, but I'm not like that. Have you been in movies?

Guy: OK, if I answer, can you tell me a little about you? I'm curious to hear about the things you like to do.

Girl: OK. You go first!

Guy: No, I'm not an actor. I'm actually a movie producer and yes I've done several movies. We're putting together a cast for a new production now, but that's business. Now tell me about you.

Notice the setup! She will probably think she'd hit gold. Who doesn't want to be in a movie? Plus, the character is genuine because there's no bragging or showing off. She dragged the information out of him. This is a flirtatious way of toying with her and setting her up for the next step. Once you feel she's on the hook and she's still trying to be good enough, then it's time to close the deal.

Case Studies (Establish Connection)
The Subway in Japan

In Tokyo they have cute little markets in the train station where they sell all kinds of trinkets, food, and drinks. We just pointed at stuff and smiled at each other—it was quite funny. The goal, however, was for her to become comfortable with me. After a few minutes, she pointed to a drink cooler. I nodded my head and she retrieved two beers. I was actually impressed by this. I paid for the beers and we strolled through the station drinking. This is actually legal in Japan. Since we were drinking, walking, and smiling, I decided it was time to do a close with her. I was convinced I'd achieved the comfort level I wanted.

On the Beach

We talked for a while about the island and its beauty and then discussed traveling in general. She'd saved money for a while and this was her big trip. As we talked, her body language showed she was comfortable with me; she played with her hair as she smiled. She sipped on a red tropical drink as we spoke, and then she sat straight to display her cleavage. It's never an accident when you get an eyeful of cleavage. Women skillfully know what they are doing and the angle they need to sit or stand to give maximum exposure. My hand gently brushed against hers and she didn't pull back. It was time to close.

At the Bar

She smiled as she assured me her colleagues would be ready to leave in half an hour. I smile back slyly. She had to return to her group, but there she was standing and talking to a man she didn't know a few minutes ago. It was time to close.

A "10" Hot Chick

We were having a great time and the place was going to close soon. Everyone was hinting they were ready to go, and two friends had already left. I believe from frustration and a last desperate attempt, she asked me to dance. I had not asked her to dance the entire night. As we danced, she pushed her body close to mine. I held her playfully, letting my hand touch her hair but nothing else. She grabbed my butt and pulled me closer as she rubbed herself on my legs. It was almost time to make the killer move.

Amateur Hour – Another "10" Hot Chick (A Failure Story)

I called her the next day and took her to an expensive dinner a few days later. We had a good time. It was a very expensive and nice restaurant. When I tried to invite myself back into her apartment after dinner, all I got was a goodnight kiss. She had to be up early the next morning.

Amateur Hour – The Nightclub Story

We started kissing as I let my hands explore her back, then her ass. She let me and it was very nice. We kissed and her hands explored me as well. I could hardly believe it. I lost track of how many songs we danced to. It could have been two or twelve. I was having a blast. I eventually touched her breast with my hands and she made no attempt to stop me. It was like we were going to make love on the dance floor. This was like a fantasy. It was really going to happen.

In the beginning it may take an

hour or two to get to this step,

but advanced students will be

able to get here within minutes.

Chapter 6
Close the Deal

CLOSE THE DEAL
- The proposal
- The seduction
- Home run

How do you get her in bed after only knowing her for a few minutes?

The prior steps were a prelude to this step. The whole thing was a setup. In the beginning it may take an hour or two to get to this step, but advanced students will be able to get here within minutes. Think of the steps as a checklist. The faster you can get through the checklist, the faster you close the deal.

Be aware that this is called a System, because if you follow each step, the full process will work. If you've come this far in the process, you are as close to a guarantee as you'll ever get in life.

The main thing to remember at this stage is that you've already established she is willing, available, and ready to go. The problem is, many women feel cheap if you say something like, "Hey, let's go back to my place and have sex." An occasional woman might find it exciting, but let's have a little class here. Also, the direct approach sometimes blows the whole deal. You've worked hard and it's now time to make the kill.

So the primary goal in this step is to give her a non-sexual reason to leave where you are and come home with you—or to her place, a hotel, etc. Several approaches will work for you at this point. The simplest is to have introduced some content into the conversation you can call on now. For instance, if I'm traveling, I might mention that the hotel where I'm staying has an amazing view of the ocean, the mountains or some other point of interest. Would she be interested in coming back to have a drink and check it out? Or, I have an interesting collection of photos I took in Paris. (I really used this one.) Would she like to check them out?

Now, women are not stupid, so they really know or suspect what you're asking. But you're making it easier for them to say yes without looking like whores or "easy" girls. Also, this keeps the mystery and confusion. She still isn't totally sure what will happen when she goes back with you. If you give her the answer to the question "Does he want to have sex with me?" then her curiosity is met, her points increase, and you go home alone. This approach gives her a clue, but keeps the game fun at the same time. It's the cat and mouse game, but the real question at this stage is who is the cat and who is the mouse?

If this is a local situation, it's always appropriate to simply ask her to come back for a drink, a glass of wine, to hang out, to see your new and beautiful house on the hill, to play video games … whatever. Just don't ask her back to have sex. That's the main and most important rule. This gives her too many points and too much power and leaves you vulnerable to rejection. If you ask her to come back for sex and she says "no," then you have a direct rejection to deal with and often there's no comeback. Many guys don't deal with rejection well. If she's asked to come back to check out your stamp collection and she says "no," then the rejection is less personal. It's easier to continue the conversation. The reason for the "no" might be that you hadn't yet established the comfort level she needed. But the "no" was not towards sex, so there's a recovery possibility. Simply continue working on the comfort level. (Go back to the previous step, mentally review other steps as well to make sure you didn't miss something.) Then make another attempt when the comfort level has been established.

This time, instead of the stamp collection, ask her to come and sample some of that imported French wine you had flown in. Don't worry, she won't be able to tell the difference when she gets there and she really won't care anyway. She didn't come home with you for the wine. I actually had a woman come home with me once with the invitation to look at some photos I took in France. We went back, had sex, had some wine, and were just enjoying the moment. I was surprised during the conversation later when she actually asked to see the photos. To her surprise, I pulled out the album with my photos of French castles and me skiing in the French Alps.

I've personally had many discussions with women who tell me this step is where many guys fail. They do everything right, but never ask her to come home with them at any point in the conversation. All the man wanted was a phone number, and she wanted sex. He never knew. And for that she didn't respect him enough to give him the right phone number. If the guy made even a feeble attempt to ask her home, many women told me they would've accepted the proposal.

Also, women will rarely make the proposal if the guy doesn't do it. Even if she's completely hot for the guy, most women feel it's *his* responsibility to ask her back home. A big mistake guys make is to ask for a phone number instead. This mistake is made because of what we discussed in Chapter 1. Men typically assume the woman will say "no" if they have just met. He believes she's a "good girl" and that asking her to come home after talking to her for a few minutes would be an insult and result in a slap in the face. That's a wrong assumption! I will only accept a phone number if I decide she's a "B" Girl and not an "A" Girl. This means that she's hot to go, but not tonight and I don't mind putting in a phone call to her in a couple days. This is OK, but the goal of the System is to get laid within minutes of meeting the girl. Any guy can get laid after a few dates, but it takes skill to get laid within minutes of meeting the woman. Learning this skill, of course, is the focus of this book.

So when should you accept a phone number? Only when you've followed all the steps and made your closing proposal once, twice, or more and she just can't go back with you. This usually happens because she's married, lives with a guy, is out with friends and can't leave them behind, has to be up at 6:00 am and it's already 1:30 am, etc. Sometimes there are legitimate reasons you have no control over. At this point it's appropriate to get a phone number or arrange to meet later that night or that week. It's best to simply change the proposal. Here are some examples:

She's with friends or her sister and doesn't want to leave with a guy she just met, but she's definitely hot for you. Or maybe she's the designated driver responsible for taking everyone home. The new proposal should be, "Hey, I could come over later after you drop them off. Why don't you just give me your address and phone number and I'll meet you in an hour at your place." You have just provided a graceful solution to her dilemma. This way she can save face with her friends, but still have fun with you.

Maybe she's married or lives with a friend and can't stay out late. New proposal: "Listen, I'm not far from here and we don't have to hang out too long. Come on, it will be fun," you say in a playful voice.

Flirt – Don't touch

This point was discussed in an earlier chapter, but it's important enough to repeat, especially at this stage. Do not try to grab tits, ass, or various other body parts of the lady while in public before having sex with her. All this does is confirm your desire for her, give her points, give her control, and screw up the deal. Flirt using the eyes, the tone of your voice, your conversation, and body language. Don't touch sexual parts, with the exception of the hands, and don't kiss until you're at a place where you can have sex. Even if she tries to kiss or be physical, play along but don't respond in turn. This will actually drive her crazy if she tries to kiss you and you politely dodge it. Your restraint will be a challenge to her. Don't be stiff and boring, but stay in control of the situation. This gives you points and takes some away from her. Remember, in many cases, once a woman confirms she can have you, she loses interest. *This rule only applies before you have sex with a woman.* After you're lovers she will find it sexy and inviting to play in public. But at this stage of the game, it's a bad thing to do.

Once you get home with her, there's no need for restraint. She will already be hot and desperate for your touch. At this point it's time for a home run.

How soon should you make the proposal to go back to your place with the girl? As soon as possible! It could take minutes or hours to get through the steps, but get her out of there as soon as possible. I call this "taking her off the market". Until she's off the market, there will be other bidders for her delights. It isn't until you have her back at your place that you can really be sure you'll get laid. The longer she's in public, the greater her chances of meeting an old friend, catching the eye of another hunter, getting too drunk, changing her mind, etc. The faster you take her off the market, the better off you'll be.

The Producer Character Close

Guy: Thanks for sharing. I can tell you're a nice person.
Girl: Thanks. You, too (while twirling her hair).

Guy: Well, listen, I wasn't going to start talking to anyone about the new production, but if you want I could have a casting session with you. No promises, but maybe you'll impress me.

Girl: No! Really?

Guy: Yeah, but I'm booked up for the next couple weeks.

Girl: (Sad look on her face)

Guy: OK. If you want we could head back to my place to do the casting. It's a simple interview, but I can't do it here. But we should go now because it's getting late.

Girl: OK. Let's go.

The Regular Guy in the Bar Close

Guy: Hey, I'm ready to head out. I'm not very far from here.

Girl: I don't know.

Guy: We'll just listen to some tunes and share a glass of wine. You're free to go whenever you want (while holding her hands in a comforting way).

Girl: OK, I guess a glass of wine isn't too bad.

Guy: No problem! Let's head out.

The Traveler

Guy: You really have to check these pictures out. The Thailand pictures are the best!
Girl: Yeah, that sounds pretty cool. Are you far from here?
Guy: No, only a few blocks. We can walk.
Girl: Right on! Let's go.

An important rule: *Don't put off for later what you can do that day or night.* This is very important to remember. It's important because women are, for the most part, unpredictable from one day to the next. The System works because you're able to establish control of the situation and environment. You're responding to an impulsive desire she has *that moment on that day*. If you take her number and let her leave without having sex with her, you'll lose control of the situation. All the rules change.

How is this possible? Let's say you follow all the steps in the System. She's hot and ready to go. But you didn't do the final step of closing. Instead, you did the amateur move and took her number to call her in two or three days as current social standards dictate. You call her in two days. She remembers you, but in a tight-lipped conversation tells you she's busy, she'll be busy this weekend, and to call her next week.

What happened? You lost control of the environment. It could have been one or a million reasons. Here are some possible reasons: an old boyfriend called her and now she can't wait to see him; she went out the next night and another guy who understood the System closed the deal with her so she's now into him; she's now on her period; she feels cheap because she met you in a bar and her social belief is that guys you meet in bars are only after 1 thing; she lost interest because she's a chick. Who knows, who cares? The bottom line is, you lost that opportunity. You wasted your time AGAIN. And you're probably calling her a bitch under your breath and kicking yourself for being stupid.

So when should you accept a phone number? Only when you've exhausted all options for that night and she's eager to give you her phone number. If you ask her for the number she says, "I don't have a phone," or "Why don't you give me your phone number and I can call you instead?" or any other excuse, simply find a polite way to thank her for the conversation and say goodbye. Giving her your phone number at that point is equal to writing you number on a piece of paper and walking over the trash bin and throwing the paper in the bin, because that's pretty much what she'll do. Girls who won't give you their number simply don't want to have sex with you. I'm sure there are exceptions, but that's all they are— exceptions. It's another rule: I never give a girl my phone number *unless* I get hers. And many times I'll take her number and not give her mine, because many girls won't call you unless you call first. Call it a chick thing, but it's true. The exception is if they are totally hot for you and YOU are not available that night. Just to frame this in context, we 're talking about first time encounters here. All the rules change after you've already had sex with the girl.

Home Run

She accepted your invitation to come back to look at your stamp collection. So what do you do now? Well, the work is already done! She's at your place, and if you really need to show her the stamp collection, you can go ahead. Offering her a drink is usually a good way to break the tension, however. Show her around the house, with the bedroom last on the tour. You want it to be last just so she doesn't ask to see the rest of the place when you're about to make your move.

This is when you satisfy her curiosity. To make clear your intentions, a touch on the arm or holding hands is a good start. If she jerks back or refuses to give you her arm, you need to work a little more on the comfort steps. Time and location are your assets. She's a captive audience. Try to find ways to make her comfortable. Ask her more about herself and what she likes to do. If you have a negative response, it's because you missed one of the steps. Your primary goal at this point is to make her comfortable and to make her trust you. Achieve this and you'll have her in bed. If you went through each step of the System successfully, a negative reaction is very unlikely at this point, however.

Assuming a positive response, here are some final closing moves:

She's standing by the sofa, the window, the balcony, etc.

Move next to her, hold her hand gently to see her reaction. If the reaction is positive, gently move you hand up and down her arm. She'll get the message. If she doesn't pull away, move closer to kiss her neck, her lips, her face. Kiss for a while, then move to her breast.

Slowly undress her as you kiss and touch her. At this point you're home free.

She's on the sofa

The steps are really the same. Touch her and watch her reaction for validation. A woman who's not interested will pull away or stiffen up. Continue touching her gently as you kiss her, undress her, and make love to her. You don't need to get up and go to the bedroom to do this. Feel free to do her exactly where you are— unless you prefer the bedroom, that is.

She's in the bedroom

I hate to repeat myself, but the moves are the same. There's no trick or magic to this. All the work of identifying the right girl, creating the comfort level, and seducing her has already been done. All that's necessary at this time is to lay her down and make love to her.

Some other strategies

A favorite of a good friend of mine is the massage move. He promises her a GREAT massage. Of course, he doesn't mind helping her relax after a long day. He explains how he studied massage techniques before he changed his major to Business while in college. Massage therapists don't make that much money, he explains. He uses some jargon to explain why her muscles are so tight and says he knows exactly how to relax her. She agrees. Women love to be pampered, and massages are top on the list for pampering. He starts with the neck, down the back, the buttocks, and between the legs that are always very wet by the time he gets there. He slips his hands inside her wet panties. She never stops him, because she enjoys the treatment.

This same friend has a Jacuzzi. Whenever he's not doing deep massages, he's in the Jacuzzi. If she didn't bring a bathing suit, it's OK. He doesn't mind. The hot water from the Jacuzzi helps relax the girl. The romantic scene is enough to get her in the mood. The closure is easy at this point. He makes his move and slams a home run every time.

Case Studies (Close The Deal)
The Subway in Japan

Since I'd achieved the comfort level, it was now time to do a close. I needed to find a reason to invite her back to my place, but there was one problem: I didn't speak enough Japanese to even say hello. However, body language is a beautiful thing. I pointed toward the direction I wanted to go, and she followed. We walked towards the exit leading from the train station towards my apartment. She went with me. We smiled and made further attempts to communicate; both of us were having a good time.

As we entered my apartment building, she showed no sign of concern. We rode up the elevator to my apartment and entered. I turned on the radio and got a couple bottles of beer. She seemed to like beer, but it didn't show on her figure—she was a skinny little thing. The girls are all tiny and beautiful in that country.

My apartment had a beautiful patio with a great view, so we stood on the patio and playfully danced for a while. I held her hand and squeezed it for reassurance. She was good to go. We kissed and then I led her back inside.

I started undressing her as we stumbled towards the bedroom.

It was great!

On the Beach

I always like to describe my hotel as a hotel with a view. That's actually true, but then every hotel has a view from the top of the building. This one was one like that. It was a budget trip and I hadn't spent a lot of cash on this place. I told her of the beautiful view from my hotel and said she just had to see it. She was curious and took me up on my offer. The hotel was only a block away. As we went up the stairs I told her I needed to stop by my room for a minute. You never need to say why. You just have a personal reason to stop by your room.

We entered my room and I asked her if she wanted a drink. They don't even have to take a sip. It could be water, soda, or alcohol. It's just a polite thing to ask and it makes them feel comfortable to have something in their hands. Also it helps with the initial transition to the new location. They feel a little more at home.

She sat on a little sofa that came with the room, more like a loveseat, which was an appropriate name. I handed her a drink, took a sip of mine, and sat on the armchair of the loveseat. I touched her shoulder with my hands, rubbing gently. She reached up with her hand and gently touched mine. I ran my hand through her hair and then leaned over and kissed her. She kissed me back. I kissed her for a while as I gently started playing with her breast. She leaned into my touch. We enjoyed each other the rest of that day and a few more times before we both headed back to our respective homes.

I don't think she ever saw the view from the top of the building. I'm not sure if she really cared.

At the Bar

It made sense to make the closing move, though we'd only been talking for less than five minutes. I told her I was staying in the hotel and asked if she wanted to stop by for a drink after she was finished with her friends. She hesitated for a moment of uncertainty. I told her the hotel had my driver's license and credit card info. If anything happened to her, they would know who I am. I think she was reassured by the comment. A girl has to be careful whom she trusts.

I gave her my room number and she agreed to stop by later. I went back to the room and took a shower. But like I said, I was tired, and I passed out the moment I hit the bed. I was awakened about 20 minutes later by the phone. She apologized for waking me up and said maybe she'd just go home. I told her it was OK, she should come on up. I was curious to know a little more about her.

She came up and didn't leave until morning. It was an amazing experience.

A "10" Hot Chick

We went back to my place after we left the club. My friends had to get their cars and everyone was hugging and kissing good night.

In front of my friends who'd bet me on this conquest I made the proposal. "You're welcome to stay here tonight. I'll take you to your hotel in the morning," was all I said to her. I held out my hand as I said the words. She looked at my buddies before reaching for my hands. I wished my friends a good night as I disappeared with the hot chick beyond my door.

It was an all-night session. She had a lot of energy and built up sexual tension, and we both had a great time. She made some wonderful comments to my friend the next time he saw her and they asked her about the experience. The boys still enjoy telling that story. The bet we made was just a friendly bet. No money exchanged hands. It was just for the challenge.

Amateur Hour – Another "10" Hot Chick (A Failure Story)

We went out a couple other times. I think I told her how beautiful she was at least a dozen times. She really was beautiful, but after a few dates we both lost some interest. She wasn't going to give it up and I got tired of spending money. We went our separate ways.

Amateur Hour – The Nightclub Story

We touched and kissed for what seemed like eternity. I was sure as anyone could be that I would get laid that night. I even slid my hands in her panties to feel her dripping wet between her legs. We stopped dancing and went back to her group, because her friends were ready to leave. I tried everything to convince her to stay and go home with me; I was practically on my knees begging. She promised to get together with me again. All I had to do was call her. I had her work number, her cell phone number, and her home number on a little bit of paper. I watched as she sped off with her girlfriends.

I called a couple of days later. We spoke briefly, but I could hear discomfort in her voice. She stated how embarrassed she was about the way she acted in the club. I could not possibly respect her. I made it clear that not only did I respect her, but also that I wanted to see her again. She said she was busy and I could call her later at home.

I called her about four other times that week, leaving messages, before giving up in frustration. She was giving me the good old dodge. She never returned any of my calls. I'd screwed up! The bird had flown the coop.

ROY VALENTINE

The purpose of a date is to have sex with her, not to impress her or finance her life.

Chapter 7
Closing on Dates

Notice that this book is not about getting dates. But for the B-Girls, the ones you didn't close on the first time you met, you *will* have to do a date thing. Here are a few basic rules for dates:

- *Don't take her out on a date.* Have the entire date at your place.
- Don't spend a lot of money on a date until after you have sex with her. This would be rewarding someone for non-performance
- If you don't close within three dates, move on. The purpose of a date is to have sex with her, not to impress her or finance her life.

Rule #1 About Dates - Don't take her out on a date.

If you have a date with a girl you've never had sex with, it's because you were not able to get her to come home with you the first time you met. If you have a date with a girl for any other reason then please go back to the first chapter of this book and re-read every page. Blind dates are the same thing: you met somewhere and you were not able to close and now you have a second date. The core principle here is that you were not able to close at the time you took her phone number and now you want another shot at it.

Given the above reason, why would you want to put yourself into another competitive environment? It's important to always be in an environment where you have the most control. This is the same rule for any competitive situation in life. I've watched friends do this with pain. They meet a girl, they aren't able to close, they call her a few days later and then invite her to go out to a nightclub with them on Friday or Saturday night. In other words it's like saying, "Hey darling, would you like to go somewhere where you can have your highest points, spend my money, and I can compete with every other guy for your attention? I'll pay for dinner, pay for you to get in the club and pay for all your drinks, and at the end of the night you can kiss me on the cheek and say how nice a guy I am?" This is of course a great deal for a girl. But for a guy it makes no sense.

Guys should set up dates in an environment where they have NO competition, where they can be the hero, and where they can have the maximum amount of romance necessary to get the panties off. There is no better place to do this than your very own castle, your cave, your domain—your home.

So is it hard to convince a woman to come home with you on a first date? Actually, it's easier than asking her to go to see a movie. Why? Because women's interest lies in the attention and romance you give them. If it's possible for her to get ALL your attention and to have a romantic experience, she will have a hard time refusing the opportunity. This is true especially since you already followed the System outlined above. You've established that she's interested in you, and she's at least curious to see where this can go.

To have the date at your place, create a romantic evening where she will be the focus of the attention. It's good to know how to cook at least one meal. Taking the time to learn how to cook one meal will open the door to more sex than most men can imagine. The fact is that most women have never had a guy cook for them. A woman finds it more romantic when a guy cooks a nice meal for her than when she's taken out to an expensive restaurant. This is very true. Instead of saying, "Hey let's go on a date to the nightclub or to the amusement park," say "How about if I make you a nice dinner. Do you like Spanish food?" Of course the answer will be a big "YES!" A good follow-up would be, "My grandmother is from Spain and this recipe was passed down for several generations." It doesn't really matter if you grandmother is from Brooklyn and you learned the recipe from the Internet. What you've done is create a romantic fantasy for her. She'll tell all her friends and thank you for the experience. Other romantic fantasies surrounding food could be, "I learned this while backpacking through India (if the meal is Indian). I helped a poor family and they invited me to dinner and this is where I learned how to make this meal." Whatever the story is, think of a good one to support the meal.

Here's a sample dialogue on the phone arranging the date.

Guy: Yes, I think it would be nice to see you again. Are you available on Wednesday?

(Never ask when she's available. Suggest a day you're most available.)

Girl: Yes, Wednesday's good.

Guy: Great, we can grab something to eat or *(pause for effect),* well .. do you like Cuban food? *(Suggest an ethnic country you think may sound exotic to her.)*

Girl: I've never had Cuban food before.

Guy: Oh you'll love it. It's hard to find a good Cuban restaurant in this town though. Listen, if you like we can go somewhere, but I have a great recipe passed down from my great grandmother who was a refugee from Cuba. I'll have to tell you how she escaped to America over the meal. What do you think? I'd love to make you dinner if you're up to it.

Girl: Wow, you know how to cook?

Guy: Of course! I promise you a feast.

Girl: Yeah, that sounds pretty nice.

Guy: Good, so Wednesday it is, about 7:30?

Girl: Yeah!

Guy: OK. Let me tell you how to get here.

At this time, give her the relevant information and get off the phone. There's no point in having an extended conversation beyond this point. You've achieved your goal. Further conversation may diminish her curiosity about you or give you an extended opportunity to put your foot in your mouth. Wish her a good night and go and practice how to cook any dish. Don't worry! She won't know the difference. It's important however to learn an exotic name for the dish. For instance, chicken with rice should NEVER be called chicken with rice on your date. Anyone can make chicken with rice. On your date it is called *arroz con pollo* (for Cuban or other Latin meals) or *poulet avec du riz* (for French-based cultures).

Remember that romance is simply a woman's fantasy. It's the name of the meal, the environment, your company, and conversation - including the story about the meal that she will find romantic, not necessarily the meal itself. Chicken and rice are the same in every country but a good story and an exotic name for the meal make it a romantic evening. Plus the fact that you are making this effort for her will give her no hesitation to take off her panties for your pleasure

About wine

Never use a domestic wine on a date. It makes no sense. An imported wine costs about $1 or $2 more than domestic wines, but you get a lot more mileage out of it. Don't worry about the quality of the wine. Some refined women will know the name and quality of the domestic wines (many have visited Napa Valley and consider themselves experts), but most of them will know nothing about wine from other countries. Go out to the liquor store or supermarket and look for something from Italy, France, Australia, Germany, etc. Compare prices and get the cheapest one. You will probably spend about $7 to $10 for the bottle.

Why is this important? Because girls are impressed by things they associate with wealth and class. Rice and chicken with beer just is not the same as *poulet avec du riz avec Beaujolais*. That's French for chicken and rice and wine. Beaujolais is an inexpensive red French wine similar to merlot.

The total cost of this French dinner for two is about $15. The same meal and wine in a French restaurant is about $70 to $100.

Real men don't cook

I was told by a friend that many men have an issue with this approach because they're either too lazy or they don't cook. I present the question then: If you knew that this approach would ALWAYS get you laid, would it be worth your effort to learn how to cook one meal? It takes 10 minutes to 20 minutes to cook most meals from any culture. It takes exactly five minutes to cook the perfect shrimp. Women tend to like seafood very much. Shrimp and lobster are some favorites. These meals take only minutes to prepare, are a fraction of the cost of restaurants, and fulfill her romantic fantasy. Recipes can be found for free on the Internet or purchased in bookstores. I even included some of my favorite recipes at the end of this chapter. The recipe tells you EXACTLY what to do and in what quantities. If you want someone to teach you, just ask you mother, your sister, or a friend that knows how to cook. All you need is one recipe. That's all it takes. Cooking for a woman who has come to your house on a date is what I call the

GUARANTEED PANTY DROPPER. It just never fails.

The main point is to have a captive audience on this date. Invite her over, make a good meal, have wine, a few lit candles, some romantic music . . . a single rose is nice, but not necessary. Don't start cooking until she's there. Take your time chopping vegetables and cooking the meal to enhance the experience for her. A big part of the event is for her to see you making the meal for her. You are making an extra effort for her pleasure. She will thank you in multitudes for this experience. Keep the conversation light and fun while you're cooking to create a fun connection. Use the information in the previous chapter about flirting. Touching and kissing are definitely allowed here. You're the king at your castle and you're entertaining your princess for the night. Relax and have fun with it. With good conversation, good food, and a comfortable, relaxed environment you just can't fail. When you finish eating the meal (or maybe even before), don't be surprised if *she* attacks you.

While cooking or eating it's good to touch, kiss, and flirt. Women find this romantic. Many times you may actually have sex while the meal is cooking. The atmosphere will be very romantic for her and sexually charged for you. You will have a captive audience for your seductive pleasure.

Here are some things to consider for home date:

- Turn off all phones in the house. Your mom, your best friend, work or someone you can't easily hang up on will almost certainly call just when you're making your move.
- Clean your house/apartment, especially your kitchen and bathroom. Women tend to notice these things and it can be a turn-off if you live like a pig.
- Let her help cut vegetables or stir the pot or something if she wants to help. It helps her feel like it's a sharing moment.
- Don't let her do the dishes, even though she may ask. Move directly from the table to the sofa where you can go for the close. Doing dishes after the meal distracts from what you should be doing, which is getting her panties off.
- Have romantic, soft music in the background. This is good for setting the mood.

- Have a few lit candles on the dinner table.

How about Eating Out?

But what if she said no to the invitation for you to cook for her? Well the proposal should have been … "I could make you a nice romantic dinner. I learned the recipe from my great grandmother (violins playing in the background) or we can go to a restaurant somewhere." Don't let the "or we can go to a restaurant somewhere" sound too romantic, since this is not the option you want her to pick. If she picks the restaurant option, you're probably not in a good situation. You have not achieved the comfort level required as yet. You have a lot more work to do. But let's assume she chose Option B – the restaurant. You should have a local restaurant already selected near your home. The end result is the same. You want to have an easy transition back to your place (or hers).

The best places are small, romantic, mom/pop hole-in-the-wall places. If it's clear she wants the restaurant option, then you can sell the mom/pop place to her. It could be something like this: "Hey, there's a cool little place that makes great Italian food. It's authentic .. blah, blah, blah..." You should know three choices within a few miles, or preferably walking distance from your castle. The distance from your home will become very important when you do your close at the end of the meal. The close is the same as listed above. Make a non-sexual proposal to come back to your place. You live five minutes away and she just has to see your view of the city. If she's interested, she will accept. If not, maybe it's time to move on.

A note about location

Most wild animals that are great hunters hunt close to home. Why? Because you have a shorter distance to take your kill home at the end of a successful hunt. What does this mean? Some of the best places to meet girls are small bars in your neighborhood or at malls or at local events. It would be sad to meet a girl then try to convince her to drive two hours back to your place only to get shot down because of the distance. If you're hunting far from home, getting a motel for that night is not a bad idea. If you're traveling, staying in a hotel in the city or near the city center is better from a location point-of-view. In Europe, every city has a *center* where everything happens. This is the place to stay—where the action is. It's a lot easier to close when you can walk back to your home or drive five or 10 minutes back to your cave with your prize for the night. Also, if you go on a date, select a restaurant close to your home so that it's an easy transition back to your place without having to drive to another city. And I'm sure I don't have to say this, but I will – never bring a friend on a date with you. That's just plain stupid.

Rule #2 About Dates - Don't spend a lot of money

I've never seen a connection between spending a lot of money on a date and getting laid. In fact, some women will think you're pretentious by throwing around too much money. It doesn't hurt to imply or hint that you're well off, but there's really no need to go beyond that. The hint creates a curiosity that she'll not get out of her head until she proves or disproves her suspicion.

Here's also what's bad about spending a lot of money on a date: You are rewarding the girl for non-performance. You're increasing her points by letting her believe she's worth all that cash even if she doesn't put out. Having champagne at your place is cool, but spending

$400 on an expensive restaurant is no more effective than a small romantic dinner. If you're wealthy, then having the dinner at your large, expensive home will definitely have a big impact. Women imagine themselves as the future woman of the house if they're taken home to an expensive home. That creates a significantly greater amount of points for you than taking her out.

After she's performed, then you want to reward her. Take her out on the town, but don't buy her anything. Let her work for her rewards. Whenever she does something exceptional, then you can spend a little cash on her to let he know your appreciation. When she doesn't put out, the rewards are taken away. Read the Pavlov dog study in your psychology books. It really works. You reward for performance, not for non-performance.

And if you don't have money and you spend a lot on a date you're creating a habit you can't sustain. Keep it simple and inexpensive.

Rule #3 About Dates – If you don't close within three dates, move on.

There should be a limit on how much abuse you will take to get into a girl's panties. Normally, if a girl is interested in you sexually and you're making an effort to get her in bed you will be able to do it within three encounters.

Again, the main goal here is to get laid. Many women support their lives via free dates with desperate men. They tease and promise, but never deliver. There's no reason to play by these rules. You aren't trying to impress her or show her how much money you can spend on her. You're simply trying to get into the panties. If she strings you along, then it's time to move on. Three dates should be the maximum opportunity she gets to show she's serious about putting out. If she has a problem with this, then she should find another sucker to milk for cash.

Also, keep in mind that each day you spend not getting laid with this woman could be spent getting laid with someone else. Chasing a woman for months when there are over two billion women in the world is ridiculous. Often this chase ends up with the guy spending lots of money, with nothing to show for it but a string of masturbation sessions after long, expensive dates.

Home Run

So you have eaten and you're back at your castle. The closing at this point is the same as described in the previous chapter. You have gotten this far in the System and all you need to do is to make your final move.

She's standing by the sofa, the window, the balcony, etc.

Move next to her, hold her hand gently to see her reaction. If the reaction is positive, gently move you hand up and down her arm. She'll get the message. If she doesn't pull away, move closer to kiss her neck, her lips, her face. Kiss for a while, then move to her breast. Slowly undress her as you kiss and touch her. At this point you're home free.

She's on the sofa

The steps are really the same. Touch her and watch her reaction for validation. A woman who's not interested will pull away or stiffen up. Continue touching her gently as you kiss her, undress her, and make love to her. You don't need to get up and go to the bedroom to do this. Feel free to do her exactly where you are— unless you prefer the bedroom, that is.

She's in the bedroom

I hate to repeat myself, but the moves are the same. There's no trick or magic to this.

ROY VALENTINE

All the work of identifying the right girl,
creating the comfort level, and seducing her has
already been done. All that's necessary at this
time is to lie her down and make love to her.

Panty-Dropping Recipes

Yes, I know that many guys don't know how to cook, don't like to cook or don't think it's worth the effort. You may be right! But I've never made dinner for a girl that I was not able to have sex with. Actually, just talking about making dinner on a date will get other girls turned on for you.

Here's a test! Have a friendly conversation with some female friends or colleagues. During the conversation mention that you love making romantic dinners for someone you date. Mention some of the meals listed below. Pay close attention to the reaction of these women. Listen to their comments.

Sharing a meal prepared by a 'love interest' is one of the most romantic times a girl can spend with a guy. The guy that provides this moment will have established himself as someone that is in a separate class from the masses.

So here are a few of my favorite Panty-Dropping recipes. I also recommend recipes from a book called *Simple & Simply Delicious* by Sylvie Rocher. I love this book because all the recipes are exotic but so simple to make that anyone can follow the instructions. Excellent!

Grilled Lobster
Homard Grille (French)

If you really want to impress her, this is the way to go. Save this one for the '10' chick though because you won't be able to get rid of her after this meal.

Ingredients:
- 2 live lobsters
- 12 ounces butter
- 6 cloves garlic (depending on taste)
- lemon wedges
- salt and pepper to taste

1. Get a large pot with a lid (be careful of the lobster claws). Put water to boil. When water is boiling (bubbling) put in live lobster (be careful if they jump). Cover lid immediately after lobster is in water. When water starts to boil again, time it for 7 minutes.
2. Rinse boiled lobster.
3. Split tails lengthwise along back.
4. Twist off head from tail. Remove liver, roe, and stomach.

5. Twist off claws where they join the body. Using a nutcracker or hammer, remove the flesh from the claws.
6. Release flesh from tails keeping end still attached. Remove intestinal vein beneath flesh of center back, rinse, and return to shell.
7. Season lightly with salt and pepper.
8. Brush generously with melted butter.
9. Turn on broiler on medium heat.
10. Place halves of lobsters, meat side up, on broiler rack.
11. Broil for 3-4 minutes or until lobsters are heated.
12. Heat remainder of butter with cloves of garlic.
13. Brush garlic butter lavishly over lobsters. Garnish with lemon wedges.
14. Serve with boiled or baked potatoes.

ROY VALENTINE

Curried Shrimp
Crevettes au Curry (French)

Every country does curry shrimp a little differently. I learned this from a young lady while backpacking in Indonesia. I could tell you what happened after the meal, but I'm sure you can guess.

Ingredients:
- 1 pound fresh shrimp, cleaned and de-veined
- 1 tablespoon butter
- 2 teaspoon lemon juice
- 2 tablespoon curry powder
- 1 onion
- 2 cloves garlic, minced
- 3 tablespoon oil
- Salt and pepper to taste

1. Sauté chopped onions and minced garlic in oil. Add curry.
2. After approximately 2 minutes, add shrimp, salt, and pepper. Cook shrimp for 5 minutes while stirring.
3. Mix in lemon juice and butter. Shrimp should be firm but tender.
4. Serve hot with white rice and tossed salad.

Mussels Steamed in White Wine
Moules Marinieres (French)

This one I got from a cute little French girl. If you haven't done Paris, you should put it on your list. But don't stay the entire time in Paris because the French countryside is a must-see experience.

Ingredients:
- 4 ½ pounds mussels
- 1 ¼ cups dry white wine
- 4 – 6 large shallots, finely chopped
- fresh parsley
- 2 tablespoon butter
- black pepper and salt to taste

1. Make sure you get fresh, cleaned mussels from the supermarket.
2. In a large pot combine the butter, garlic, and shallots. Sauté over medium heat and cook for 2 minutes.
3. Add wine, cook for 2 additional minutes.
4. Add mussels and cook, tightly covered, for 5 minutes or until the mussels open, shaking and

tossing the pan occasionally.
Discard any mussels that do not
open.

5. Add chopped fresh parsley.
6. Serve with white rice or boiled
   potatoes.

Fricasseed Chicken
Fricasse de Poulet (French)

Jamaica is a beautiful and a fun country.
This one I learned years ago from an old
Jamaican friend.

Ingredients:
- 2 to 4 pieces of chicken (breast, legs, etc.)
- 1 teaspoon of seasoned salt (I recommend Lawry's, if you can find it in your local supermarket)
- ½ teaspoon black pepper
- 3 cloves garlic, minced
- 2 tablespoon oil
- 2 cups water
- 1 tablespoon steak sauce
- ½ lb chopped potatoes
- ¼ lb diced carrots
- 1 onion finely chopped

1. Add seasoned salt, black pepper, garlic, steak sauce, and chopped onions to chicken in a bowl. Allow to marinade for 30 or more minutes.
2. Heat oil and add chicken. Brown just enough to stiffen chicken..

3. Add water, potatoes and carrots.
4. Cook on medium, covered, for 10 minutes. Simmer for 10 minutes.
5. Serve hot in gravy with rice.

Arroz con Pollo

This is a popular Spanish dish, but you can also find it in Cuba and South America. It's yellow rice mixed with chicken, topped with melted cheese. This is one of my all-time favorites.

Ingredients:
- Fricasseed chicken (see above)
- Yellow saffron rice
- Shredded cheese (you can buy it in a bag at the supermarket with multiple types of cheeses grated and mixed)

1. Cook yellow rice as instructed on package.
2. Mix chicken with rice in pot.
3. Flatten top of chicken/rice mixture.
4. Add hefty layer of shredded cheese.
5. Cover pot and simmer for 5 minutes or until cheese is melted.

ROY VALENTINE

I'm an international player.

This simply means that not only

can I have sex whenever I want,

but I can do this on a global

scale.

Chapter 8
How to Be a Player

Now that you've acquired the skills required to pick up girls, you need to learn how to be a player. A player is a guy that has a selection of girls that he can have sex with whenever he wants to have sex. On any given day or at any given time, he has sex on demand. I'm an international player. This simply means that not only can I have sex whenever I want, but I can do this on a global scale.

Successful players have two essential skills: The first is the ability to meet girls and have sex with them, which you've learned from this book. The second skill is to be able to repeatedly have sex with these girls whenever you want. This chapter will give you some guidelines regarding the second skill.

As you can tell by now, I like efficient processes. This is the same when it comes to getting laid repeatedly. A core difference between a Player and a guy who goes out to get laid and hopes to get lucky is this: The Player realizes that to have sex with a girl once and then dump her is a waste of effort. Why would you want to throw away available sex?

Instead, you need to learn how to maintain an open channel to her bed. The fact is, once you've been inside the panties there is always an open path back to it. Have you ever run across an old girlfriend or lover? Did she make it clear in her own way that the sex was still yours if you wanted it? Of course she did. Why? Because you're a known and safe commodity. You're low risk! There is already an emotional attachment. You are already at Step 4 of the System and have achieved the Comfort level without even trying.

Therefore, you're at Step 4 of the System with any girl you've already had sex with. Literally, all you have to do is give her a call, invite her over, and close. We call this a booty call.

Why are Players always confident and why do they always have hot girls with them? The fact is, they keep ex-lovers around! That's the bottom line. Imagine if you were able to pick up the phone and at random have sex with any of your ex-lovers at will. Think of the really hot girls you've done in the past. Think of the one-night stands you never called back. You've already been to the well, and you can go back at any time. To have this benefit, however, you must maintain a connection with them. Fortunately, that's easy to do.

The Benefits of Booty Call Girls

The first thing you have to understand is that girls hate one-night stands because it makes them feel like whores. It isn't only the fact that she went home with you after just meeting you that she hates. She feels used the next day when the phone doesn't ring. She feels as though she opened herself up and allowed you in and she must now be a stupid cheap whore if you haven't called. She feels stupid, and this is what pisses women off over men and one-night stands.

So, by default they actually want you to call them the next day. This, my friend, is a golden opportunity for a Player. A Player knows that a woman he has had sex with is a woman he can ALWAYS have sex with. So why not give her what she wants? If you don't call her, she'll think you're an asshole and cry herself to sleep. Sometimes she may even go into depression. If you do call her she will think you're great and not one of those other guys. Therefore, by calling her and doing her again, you are helping her out. You are actually doing *her* a favor. You are the good guy here.

So knowing this, why would you want to throw away good and available sex? It makes no sense. You've made the investment in seducing and having sex with her already. Why not reap the rewards?

Imagine being able to pick up the phone whenever you want to and invite yourself over to the home of a list of lovers. These are girls you've already had sex with. You simply choose which one you want that day. Maybe you want to watch football on Monday night and simply arrange for her to come over after the game. You have sex with her and then not see her for a week or two. There's no need to go hunting as much when you can just have the girl come to you. It makes perfect sense to me. How about you?

Or you go to the club with the boys and on your way home at 3:00 am you call from your list of booty call girls. One or two may be asleep, but there's always one who's at home and would love to have company. Which girl wants to sleep alone when she can have a lover she knows and trusts? You show up on her doorstep shortly after, and she's eagerly awaiting your arrival.

Maybe you travel on business and you have a couple of booty calls in the cities you frequent. You had a long day of meetings. You go hunting anyway on your way to the hotel and come up with nothing. It's just not happening that night. Your 1% is nowhere to be found. Hey, guess what, it's time to give your booty call a phone call. You didn't tell her you were coming to town because it was a last-minute trip and this was the first opportunity you had to call her.

Do you get it? The point is, you can still hunt for fresh meat because the only thing that's better than pussy is new pussy. But, why not have a backup plan? Don't have one booty call girl, make every girl you have sex with a booty call girl. Even if one or two of these girls are not available, you have a list of several girls to choose from. At least one or more of them will be available whenever you want to have sex. But that's only if you want to have sex from the booty call list.

How can you make every girl a booty call girl?

Women are beautiful and sensitive creatures. I love women, but I understand a core difference between men and women. I'm certainly not a psychologist, but I've had enough female friends, not just lovers, in whom I've seen an astonishing pattern. The pattern is well documented and should be common knowledge. It's this simple: Sex creates a greater emotional connection and investment for women than it does for men.

When women have sex with men they don't fall in love, but it means *something*. For every woman that something may be different. Many women who screw around a lot have a hard time dealing with it emotionally. Men typically don't have that problem. We may become bored after awhile, but most men don't even need to know the name of the woman they're having sex with. How many times has this happened? You meet a girl, you do her the same day, you try to remember her name a week later and go blank. Don't ask me to explain it, because I'm no shrink. I'm just a guy; thank God.

This little bit of information is essential because once you understand it you'll find that sleeping with a woman makes her more open to sleeping with you a second or third or infinite number of times. You had sex with her and she now has some level of emotional connection with you. It is therefore easier for you to get back into the panties than the other guy who's trying to do so for the first time.

This reason is why old boyfriends are always a threat. She may not be in love with him, but she will have some emotional connection and comfort level with him. If you had sex with her last night or last year, just pick up the phone and call her or send her an email. You're not a stranger—you're an ex-lover. The door is already open and all you have to do is walk in. In fact, if you've never done this you should call each of your ex-lovers you want to have sex with and simply ask her to meet you for a drink or coffee. After all, you were just thinking of her *'with a smile'* and you just want to see how she's doing.

Most of the time she'll say "yes." Keep the conversation short but sweet. Don't fulfill her current emotional need *(which is to be heard)* over the phone. Inquire about her life briefly, and then let her know that you'd like to hear more about what she's been up to, but you have an appointment you're late for. Can you meet later that day (or another day) to *'catch up.'* Agree on a specific date and time before getting off the phone. Don't make the meeting date too far into the future. It really should be that day or that week if possible. Don't ask her

Don't tell her you miss her.

You will have given her all the

power and control in the

situation.

to go to the nightclub or to dinner with you. Her guards will immediately go up. It will sound like a date and she will know the trick. Don't tell her you miss her. You will have given her all the power and control in the situation. Just show some interest in what's going on in her life. Unfortunately, however, *you are unavailable this minute* to hear the full story. You can however make some time to get together at some point in the very near future. If her schedule is full for the next week or two, then leave her alone and move on to happier grounds. You're just not a priority anymore in her life. Leave her your phone number and maybe she's call, but don't wait by the phone. If she does agree, then you're in. When you meet her, apply the steps of the System and you will get laid that very day or night.

For a new lover (the girl you just did yesterday), you simply need to call her and show concern. Express that you had a wonderful time, and let her know you wanted to make sure she's OK. What's she doing on Wednesday? Women are always available from Monday night to Thursday night. They have nothing to do and you won't have to compete for their time with other events in their lives.

Once you've given her a call and had sex with her again, she will expect to see you every once in awhile. That's OK. Just see her when it's convenient for *you*. Don't feel obligated to call often. A phone call or an email now and then is OK. She will want more, but don't give it to her. If you find yourself communicating with her on a daily basis, she's effectively pulling you in and you're on the path to getting a girlfriend. You don't want that—not if you want to be a player, that is. You have the rest of your life for girlfriends and wives. Right now, you need to control yourself and establish some ground rules to secure your freedom and establish that she will continue to be a booty call until *you* choose to phase out of the fold.

Underestimating Women

So if it's this easy, why doesn't every guy have a dozen or more women to choose from? The first part of that answer is lack of skill. This book teaches you some of these skills. The second part is that men underestimate women. Because of this they have sex with women and leave them. They throw away their well-earned booty. Here are some reasons why a guy never calls back a girl after a one-night stand:

- He feels guilty because he thinks he just used her.
- He thinks she may want more in terms of a relationship.
- He thinks she's cheap or easy if she had sex with him after just meeting him.
- The challenge is gone. Time to move on to new opportunities.

Each of these reasons comes from different mental states of a guy. Depending on the man's experience and belief system, the reasons will change.

He feels guilty because he thinks he just used her.

Men grow up believing we should be serious about every woman we sleep with. We believe that if we aren't serious and have sex just for the sake of having sex, we're using the woman. We're taught to be compassionate, loving, and caring to women, which I am. We're taught to be respectful of her needs and desires, which I am. We believe we should do this to the exclusion of our own needs and desires – which I don't agree with. These values are good. I certainly love and respect women. I treasure women and I treasure the love of someone dear to me above all else. I am compassionate and caring to all women. And it is because of this that I think these women deserve a chance to get to know me better. It's because of this they get a shot at finding their partner. It's possible I could be that person, or I may not be. Therefore, as she seeks to discover whether or not she's found a match to fulfill her needs, is it unfair that I should have my needs fulfilled as well? Her primary need may be to find a partner, but my primary need, as a man is to have sexual fulfillment. Both needs can be satisfied simultaneously.

He thinks she wants more in terms of a relationship and he doesn't.

Women are ALWAYS on automatic pilot to find Mr. Right. So, yes, if you happen to be a good lover, a great guy, and a fun dude—you'll probably be put on her list of potential partners. But that's her problem! Don't make it yours. Tell her you enjoy her company, but that you don't want a relationship with her. See her and have sex with her only when it suits you. Don't get serious with her unless you want to. Here's a way you can break it to her after having sex with her a few times.

Girl: So what are you doing this weekend?

Guy: Hanging out with some friends on Saturday. I'm available Friday if you want to get together.

Girl: Which friends? Where are you going? *(This is the first step to female control over guys. Use it as a golden opportunity.)*

Guy: Hey, I really think you're cool and we have a great time together, but *(pause for effect)* I have different friends I hang out with. I guess we should talk about expectations and relationships. I just like to be honest and upfront so we don't have any confusion between us. Are you looking for a long-term relationship? *(Now she's caught off-guard and has to respond.)*

Girl: Well, not really, I mean, we just met.

Guy: Good, because I think relationships are important and I think it's very important to get to know someone before making a long-term commitment. Until then, however, I won't consider anything exclusive.

Girl: Yeah, me too.

Guy: Great!

At this point you switch the conversation to more pleasant topics. She has agreed to a non-exclusive arrangement and there's no point in trying to explain or justify things any further. She has just agreed to be your booty call. The more you talk, the more you will have to explain. This is the time to ask if she wants something to drink or simply ask her about her day at work or school.

He thinks she's cheap or easy if she had sex with him after just meeting him.

If women were easy there would never be a need for books like this one. Every guy would be having sex with a different girl everyday. It's cultural or religious programming that links getting a girl to bed with little effort to the actual value or morals of the woman. It's this belief that prevents you from creating the comfort level required to get girls to bed effortlessly. Because of this judgmental attitude girls are forced to say "NO" when they'd like to say "YES." They can read that judgmental attitude and they will shy away from you. If she says "NO," she's a bitch. If she says "YES," she's a whore. You give her no winning options. This single belief will send you home alone and set you up for abuse.

Abuse? Yes! Because, some women will recognize your naïveté and realize you're looking for the "Good Girl." She will hold out on having sex for as long as she can, while she may be having sex with another guy. You will be the clueless idiot. She'll milk you for cash, gifts, and favors. She knows the moment she gives you sex, she loses you. Because the moment she gives you sex, she's a bad girl or a whore in your eyes.

Control your mind and realize that girls love sex as much as men. That doesn't make her a whore—it makes her human. The man who understands this and encourages her sexuality instead of suppressing it will enjoy sexual experiences beyond his fantasies.

The challenge is gone. Time to move on to new opportunities.

Many men have this problem. Once the conquest is done, it's time for the next girl. There's nothing wrong with that, but it isn't efficient. Keep some on the side as booty calls and tap that ass now and then for sport. Think of it as helping the needy or a community service. If you weren't there, what would she be doing with herself?

Rules of the Player

Like everything else, you need to have a basic set of rules or guidelines to follow. These guidelines are good because they provide the answers before the questions. Think of walking into a test where the teacher put all the answers on the board. Could you fail the test?

Here are the rules Players must live by. Violate these rules and you'll have problems you just don't want to deal with.

1. Never refer to a booty call as your girlfriend, either publicly or privately.
2. Never allow her to live with you longer than a weekend.
3. Never trust her when she says she's on the pill or that she's using protection.
4. Never see her more than two times per week.
5. Never give her unrestricted access to you.
6. Never agree to an exclusive relationship with her.
7. Only lie when it's absolutely necessary.
8. Never physically or emotionally abuse her.
9. Be her super lover.

Never refer to her as your girlfriend.

She's not your girlfriend. She's a lover, a booty call; she's available sex. If she wants to become a girlfriend she should earn the right to that title through time and patience. If you refer to her even once as a girlfriend, she will never forget it. If you say she's your girlfriend and you have sex with someone else she will make you feel like shit.

You are not her boyfriend, so that makes you a free agent. If the topic comes up, confidently and without hesitation tell her she's a very nice girl and you like her, but you're not interested in an exclusive arrangement. Tell her if she isn't comfortable with that you will understand. She will not leave. If she believes you're her boyfriend, however, and you say the same words, she'll think you have cheated on her and she will never forgive you.

The booty call list is really for times when you feel too lazy to go out and find fresh new girls. Football night is a good night, but Sundays are also good. Sunday is a day of rest so I like to take Sundays off and spend some quality time with family, friends, or one of the booty call steadies.

Never allow her to live with you more than a weekend.

The goal of women is to get you into a relationship. The goal of men is to get sex. It's a fascinating game. Women realize that by living with you they achieve their goal instantly. This is a major play on their part. If a woman lives with you she has effectively blocked all other women from getting close to you. She controls the bed, the telephone, the house, and your cock. You will need to get permission to have women over and will have a fight every time you do.

Also, once they're in, it takes an act of God to get them out. Be careful of this one. This is like the Jedi trick of women. They have a dramatic or good reason why they should move in and why that would make you the hero. They promise the situation is temporary, only for a few weeks until they get on their feet or something like that. After the promised time has passed you can't kick them out because that would make you an asshole. Next thing you know, you have a live-in girlfriend. You were warned!

Never trust her when she says she's using protection.

As a general rule, you must understand that if a woman really wants to keep you she will do almost anything to achieve this goal. If you're a Player, she may just believe she's the one who can let you see the light. She can change or convert you to become an upstanding citizen and the father of her child. Don't give her the chance.

If you're a Player you have all the selections you want. It would be a painful situation to have to look into some girl's eyes as she tells you she's pregnant. "Pregnant! But you said you were on the pills," may be your reaction. Too late dude, she's got you and there's nothing you can do about it. You've been played.

Use a condom and never trust chicks. They lie, they lie, and they lie. Also, don't trust your judgment. You already know once the panties come off which head will be doing the thinking. Just make it a rule. Make an investment in some condoms and don't fall for an old trick.

You should also use condoms to protect yourself from sexually-transmitted diseases (STDs). Check out the American Social Health

Association (ASHA) or other sites for more info about STDs. Visit their site at http://www.ashastd.org/stdfaqs/. Play, but play safely.

Never see her more than twice per week.

Seeing her once per week is a booty call. Seeing her twice per week is dangerous. Seeing her three or more times per week is definitely a relationship. If you want a relationship, seeing her that many times is cool. If you just want to get laid then there's no reason to give her that much time. Cycle your time between your other booty calls and your new conquests. Don't get hooked until you're ready. Because if you do, the next thing you know, you'll have to call her every day to account for your whereabouts.

Never give her unrestricted access to you.

It should be made clear that as much as you enjoy her company she should call *before* coming over. You are not always open for visitors. You have an active life and value your privacy. If she wants to ensure she's able to spend quality time with you, she should plan ahead. Recommend that she call you a few days beforehand to make plans. It's only respectful of your time for her to do so.

If you allow her to come by whenever she wants, it's only a matter of time until she walks in on you doing some other girl. Even though she knows she's not your girlfriend, it's never a pretty sight to get caught with your pants down. Let's avoid the conflict. Just knowing she doesn't have unrestricted access to you will drive her insane. She'll do anything to get on your preferred list and win you over the other girls she suspects you're seeing. What you do whenever she's not with you is your own business. You never have to justify the way you spend your private time and with whom you spend that time.

Never agree to an exclusive relationship with her.

Her primary goal will be to achieve lockdown. This is in her best interests because she knows it keeps the competitors away. It won't be long before she tries to get you to commit to being her boyfriend or to some other exclusive arrangement. Don't do it! You don't have to. The greater you resist commitment, the harder she will try. It becomes a challenge to many girls to lock down the guy they're interested in.

Simply let her know you aren't against long-term relationships, but you need a lot of time to determine if someone is right for you. Until then, you prefer to keep the situation non-exclusive. If she isn't willing to take the time to know you before jumping into a commitment then maybe it's just not meant to be. You have to present that argument in a way that makes her seem desperate if she just wants to jump into a relationship without "really getting to know you." It works every time.

Only lie when it's absolutely necessary.

I never lie to women! There's never a reason to. When you lie, you have put the burden of the relationship and her feelings and her life on your back. Don't lie; tell her the truth. Push it back on her. If she asks where you were when she tried to reach you on Saturday night at 3:00 am, tell her you were partying with a friend or that it's none of her business. She's not your girlfriend. You have no moral obligation to justify how you spend your time to her. If you start lying, you give her the control and power. You will find yourself lying about everything. Also, lying assumes she can't handle the truth. You may be surprised just how cool some chicks can be. Why run around lying and feeling guilty when you don't have to? After all, you're a free man.

Never physically or emotionally abuse her.

Players don't beat up women. Bullies and cowards do. I am 100% against all types of abuse to women. I think it's wrong, cowardly, and not necessary. If you are ever pushed to the point of anger that you want to hit her, just leave. Be smart – be a man!

Be her super lover.

You need to be able to get her hooked on sex like it was a drug. Give her multiple orgasms every time you see her. Create an exciting sexual or romantic adventure each time you are with her. Do her in the park, on the balcony, at the beach, in her office, etc. Keep it intense! Every time she thinks about you she should become sexually excited. You must know how to tease her and please her, both sexually and emotionally. To be a true Player, you need to know these skills.

Help a Friend

It took me a lot of effort and analysis to figure out how to get the results that I do now from women. At first I thought every other guy knew this stuff but learned that very few men do.

Please help a friend by recommending this book to them. It could make the difference in their life that I hope it will in yours.

Let's Talk

I would like to know what you think of the book and your experiences or results from the book. Also share your ideas and learn more from me personally and others. Do online reviews, blogs, or send me an email. I do read all emails, blogs and reviews. You can find me at:

My Blog
http://royvalentine.blogspot.com

My Website
www.royvalentine.com

My Email Address
royvalentine@eyecontactmedia.com